THE TIES
THAT BLIND

HOW THE U.S.-SAUDI
ALLIANCE DAMAGES
LIBERTY AND SECURITY

THE TIES
THAT BLIND

TED GALEN CARPENTER
and MALOU INNOCENT

CATO
INSTITUTE
WASHINGTON, D.C.

Content in this publication originally appeared in *Perilous Partners: The Benefits and Pitfalls of America's Alliances with Authoritarian Regimes*, by Ted Galen Carpenter and Malou Innocent. Copyright 2015.

ISBN 978-1-948647-41-0   hardback
ISBN 978-1-948647-39-7   paperback
ISBN 978-1-948647-40-3   ebook

Cover design: Jon Meyers.
Printed in the United States of America.

CATO INSTITUTE
1000 Massachusetts Ave., N.W.
Washington, D.C. 20001
www.cato.org

Contents

Introduction: An Already Poisonous Relationship Gets Even Worse

The murder of Saudi journalist Jamal Khashoggi has cast a deep shadow over Washington's close military and political relationship with Saudi Arabia. Riyadh's ever-changing story about how Khashoggi died undermines that government's already weak credibility, and it confirms the kingdom's well-deserved reputation for extreme human rights abuses. The account from Turkey's intelligence service of what happened after Khashoggi entered the Saudi consulate in Istanbul—with graphic descriptions of torture, murder, and possible dismemberment—has justifiably horrified populations and governments around the world.

Yet the Trump administration's initial reaction to the incident took the Saudi regime's explanations seriously and seemed designed to sweep the problem under the rug. Secretary of State Mike Pompeo paid an immediate visit to Riyadh for talks with Crown Prince Mohammed bin Salman, even though evidence already indicated that he was the person responsible for Khashoggi's assassination. The meeting was cordial and indicated that the killing might become nothing more than a minor glitch in the longtime bilateral relationship.[1] Indeed, President Donald Trump repeatedly emphasized the importance of Washington's ties to Saudi Arabia, including citing the (exaggerated) value of the kingdom's purchases of American-made weapons and overall bilateral commerce.[2] Only when evidence continued to mount about the Saudi regime's (and specifically, Bin Salman's) complicity, did the Trump administration's criticisms begin to sharpen.

The administration's initial reaction was indicative of the willingness of U.S. leaders throughout more than seven decades to overlook or even excuse Riyadh's execrable domestic and international conduct in order to preserve close ties. Washington's solicitous, even enabling, posture toward Saudi Arabia cannot disguise the fact that the kingdom has never been a reliable U.S. ally. Indeed, it has been

1

a thoroughly duplicitous one. Continuing to collaborate with that country cannot be justified even on strategic grounds. It certainly cannot be justified on moral grounds.

Khashoggi's murder—as appalling as it was—is hardly the only instance of Riyadh's violent elimination of regime critics. On January 2, 2016, the government executed prominent Shiite cleric Nimr Baqir al-Nimr for alleged terrorist activities. Indeed, Nimr may have been the most prominent critic of the royal family to be expunged before the Khashoggi episode.[3] In addition to executing Nimr, the government also had sentenced to death his 17-year-old nephew, Ali Mohammad Baqir al-Nimr, for daring to participate in pro-democracy demonstrations that the Arab Spring had spawned throughout the Middle East. Only a concerted international campaign has caused the Saudi government to refrain from executing the incarcerated younger Nimr—so far.

Numerous opponents who are less renowned have not been so lucky. Indeed, Riyadh's per capita use of capital punishment rivals only that of China and Iran. The regime executed 146 people in 2017 and is on pace for a similar total in 2018. Although some of the individuals were accused of murder and similar heinous crimes, others clearly were silenced political dissenters. Indeed, several of the victims in recent years were people who merely participated in the Arab Spring pro-democracy demonstrations or who dared to criticize regime policies. Moreover, in addition to such political "crimes," capital offenses in Saudi Arabia include adultery, atheism, sorcery, and witchcraft.[4] Execution methods achieve impressive heights of barbarism and sadism. Not only does the government behead prisoners—a practice the United States and its Western allies vehemently condemn when the Taliban and the Islamic State have done so—but it also crucifies some defendants charged with capital crimes. Amnesty International's 2017–2018 report confirms that Saudi Arabia continues to amass an appalling record on human rights.[5]

Khashoggi's murder merely illustrates the kingdom's extensive record of human-rights abuses and outright war crimes. The latter is apparent in the way Riyadh has conducted the war in Yemen. There is abundant evidence of multiple atrocities that Riyadh and its United Arab Emirates (UAE) junior partner have committed and continue to commit in that conflict.[6] The coalition's war strategy has created a famine as well as a cholera epidemic.[7] Among the many deliberate attacks on innocent Yemeni civilians was an August 2018 incident in which coalition aircraft attacked a school bus, killing 40 children.[8]

Yet, incredibly, just weeks after that horrific incident, Secretary Pompeo certified that Saudi and UAE forces were making a reasonable attempt to avoid inflicting harm on civilians.[9] Pompeo's certification was necessary to meet the requirements of a congressional statute barring aid, especially military aid, to countries that do not take appropriate precautions. The latest certification preserves the fiction that Saudi and UAE forces are not guilty of war crimes and that the United States is not a willing accomplice in such crimes.[10]

Unfortunately, Washington has been deeply involved in assisting the Saudi war effort since Riyadh initiated its intervention in the spring of 2015. American defense firms (with the U.S. government's blessing) supply coalition forces with most of the bombs and missiles that it uses in the Yemen conflict. In addition, the United States actively assists the war effort by giving key military intelligence to Saudi and UAE forces and refueling coalition combat aircraft.

Washington offers two justifications for providing such support. One is that Saudi Arabia and its partners are merely responding to Iran's previous interference in Yemen, whereby Tehran is attempting to install its Shiite co-religionists, the Houthis, in power. Credible experts have effectively debunked that rationale, pointing out that Yemen's internal factionalism long predated any moves by Tehran; Iran's meddling before the Saudi-led intervention was minimal; and there are major differences, both in religious doctrine and political objectives, between the Houthis and the Iranians.[11] Moreover, even if Iran has interfered in Yemen's internal affairs, that action did not justify the much larger, more brazen, Saudi intervention—much less justify the accompanying and ever-worsening list of war crimes.

The second justification that terrorist groups, especially al Qaeda in the Arabian Peninsula (AQAP), have infiltrated Yemen—does not hold up much better. Houthi and AQAP forces have clashed on numerous occasions.[12] That development is not surprising, because al Qaeda is a staunchly Sunni Muslim organization, whereas the Houthis are at least a Shiite offshoot. By supporting Riyadh's crusade against the Houthi faction, the United States actually is helping to weaken one of AQAP's principal adversaries.

If Saudi Arabia were truly an essential and loyal U.S. ally, a plausible argument could be made that Americans would just need to hold their collective noses about the regime's moral outrages and preserve the alliance in the name of defending vital American security interests.[13] Realists understand that moral compromises must be made at times. Henry Kissinger emphasized that point. "A country that demands moral perfection in its foreign policy," he observed, "will achieve neither perfection nor security."[14]

There have been times when even ethical, democratic societies have had to submerge their moral qualms when vital security interests were at stake. Thus, during World War II, the governments of the United States and Great Britain were willing to forge the Grand Alliance with Joseph Stalin's Soviet Union, one of the most brutal, repulsive political systems in modern history. The alternative seemed to be the risk of defeat at the hands of Nazi Germany and its allies.

But such truly existential threats are rare. Unfortunately, U.S. leaders both during and after the Cold War have been much too willing to make moral compromises when the interests at stake are far more modest. Abandoning essential moral standards and values for the defense of lesser interests is never justified. Yet that is what the United States has done regarding its relationship with Saudi Arabia for decades.

The extent of genuine American interests in the Middle East is debatable. Defenders of Washington's longstanding relationship with Saudi Arabia (and other authoritarian Middle Eastern countries) contend that protecting a cheap and reliable oil flow from the region is essential to the global economy. As discussed in the original chapters from my 2015 book *Perilous Partners*, that justification was exaggerated even when Washington feared that its superpower adversary might gain control over the oil supply.[15] But such a (remote) possibility disappeared when the Soviet Union dissolved at the end of 1991. With the emergence of significant producers in other regions and the dramatic boost in America's own output, that rationale now lacks all credibility.

Washington's other justifications for maintaining the Saudi alliance also are strained and uncompelling. Maintaining those ties in the name of promoting greater regional stability has done the opposite. Washington's military interventions in Iraq and Syria (with enthusiastic Saudi prodding in both cases) may well have weakened two regimes that Riyadh detested, but the outcome has been greater chaos and human suffering, not greater stability. Partnering with an ultra-autocratic government like that of Saudi Arabia in the name of promoting a "freedom agenda" for the Middle East, as George W. Bush touted and Barack Obama implicitly embraced, was bitterly ironic and inappropriate.

The reality is that the United States has no truly vital interests in the Middle East that warrant the kind of distasteful moral compromises that are inherent in maintaining an alliance with Saudi Arabia. And invoking the cynical justification that the Saudis are good customers for American goods and that they create jobs for U.S. firms is beyond the pale.

Contrary to the image that Saudi leaders—and too many U.S. officials, think tank scholars, and media pundits—have fostered, Saudi Arabia is not a loyal ally helping to advance crucial U.S. interests in the Middle East and the broader Muslim world. Instead, Riyadh has consistently engaged in actions that undermined America's security and strengthened extremist factions, sometimes even outright terrorist elements. The war in Yemen is not the only instance in which the United States has allowed itself to be manipulated by Riyadh for the kingdom's dubious, parochial purposes. Indeed, as these pages show, Saudi officials have played a succession of U.S. administrations like a geopolitical violin.

As far back as the 1980s, when the United States and Saudi Arabia were supposedly on the same side helping the Afghan mujahideen resist the Soviet army of occupation, Saudi officials worked closely with Pakistan's intelligence agency to divert the bulk of U.S. financial and military aid to the most radical Islamist forces. Some of those recipients even became cadres in terrorist organizations around the world once the war in Afghanistan ended.[16]

Saudi Arabia's support for extremists in Afghanistan was consistent with its overall policy. For decades, the Saudi government has funded the outreach program of the Salafist "Wahhabi" clergy and its fanatical message of hostility to secularism and Western values generally. Training centers (madaris) have sprouted like poisonous ideological mushrooms in portions of the Muslim world thanks to Saudi largesse. That campaign of indoctrination has had an enormous impact on at least the past two generations of Muslim youth. Given the pervasive program of Saudi-sponsored radicalism, it is no coincidence that 15 of the 19 hijackers on 9/11 were Saudi nationals.

More recently, Riyadh has backed some of the most extreme elements among Syrian insurgents attempting to overthrow Bashar al-Assad's regime.[17] A prominent, well-funded, and well-armed Saudi surrogate is Ahrar al-Sham, an organization that embraces a Salafist orientation very similar to Saudi Arabia's religious dogma. One of Ahrar al-Sham's closest allies in the anti-Assad insurgency has been Jabhat al-Nusra, which until 2016 was al Qaeda's Syrian affiliate—and its largest affiliate in any country. Although Nusra has changed its name to Hayat Tahrir al-Sham and supposedly severed its connection with al Qaeda, it remains as radically Islamist as ever. Moreover, the two Syrian radical groups still maintain close military cooperation in their increasingly desperate effort to salvage the reeling Syrian rebellion. Because both the Obama and Trump administrations have insisted that the United States wants to back only "moderate" insurgents seeking to bring a democratic government to power in Syria, collaborating with Saudi Arabia and its clients is a curious way to pursue that objective.[18]

A prominent motive for Washington's continuing collaboration with Saudi Arabia is a shared antipathy toward Iran. The United States needs to overcome its obsessive hostility toward that country. The reflexive animosity already has impelled the Trump administration to repudiate the Joint Comprehensive Plan of Action—the valuable multilateral agreement designed to contain Tehran's nuclear program.[19] Mutual hostility toward Iran now appears to be the last-ditch justification defenders use for preserving the U.S. alliance with Saudi Arabia, but it is as insufficient as all the other excuses.

Granted, Iran's government is a nasty, repressive regime. Reports from Amnesty International, Human Rights Watch, and other organizations over the years, though, confirm that there is little difference in the human-rights records of Iran and Saudi Arabia. Where there are modest differences—for example, regarding the rights of women—Iran fares noticeably better. The same is true of political pluralism; Iran is less regimented than its regional rival. Although far from being a democracy, Iran does have elections with candidates representing opposing views. Current President Hassan Rouhani was elected from a multicandidate field in 2013 and secured re-election in May 2017 against a significantly more hardline candidate. There is nothing even remotely comparable to such political or ideological competition in Saudi Arabia. Likewise, although U.S. officials are fond of saying that Iran is the world's chief sponsor of terrorism, Riyadh's cozy relationship with violent Islamist groups in multiple countries indicates that Saudi Arabia deserves that title at least as much.

Washington's obsession with undermining Iran may be the principal glue holding the U.S.-Saudi alliance together, but that relationship repeatedly puts the United States in awkward and sometimes morally indefensible positions.[20] It is strikingly hypocritical for U.S. leaders to accuse Iran of interfering in the internal affairs of neighboring countries but then excuse Saudi Arabia's military intervention in Bahrain in early 2011 to keep the autocratic Sunni monarchy in power against the wishes of the majority Shiite population. Fear that a new Shiite-led government would become an Iranian pawn impelled the Obama administration to adopt that stance. Similar fear that a Houthi government in Yemen would help tilt the regional balance of power in favor of Iran is a major reason why both the Obama and Trump administrations have backed the Saudi-led war effort, despite the profusion of coalition war crimes.

Instead of trying to manage the turbulent politics of the Middle East, the United States needs to reduce its own political and military profile in that region. America has no interests at stake that are sufficiently central to warrant continuing to back a duplicitous, self-serving, and morally odious regime like that of Saudi Arabia. Cato Institute Research Fellow Emma Ashford correctly assesses the current environment. "Unlike past decades," she contends, "U.S. leaders today don't have to tolerate" objectionable Saudi behavior. "A less friendly relationship with Saudi Arabia won't harm U.S. interests in the Middle East. It's time to stop turning a blind eye to the worst excesses of the Saudi leadership."[21]

Indeed, Washington needs to terminate the alliance with Riyadh and adopt a new wary, arms-length relationship with that country and with the region. The current policy cannot be justified on either strategic or moral grounds.

The following two chapters, excerpted from my book *Perilous Partners*, coauthored with Malou Innocent, document the many instances in which U.S. and Saudi interests diverged. Combined with the recent cases discussed here, the case for terminating the toxic U.S.-Saudi alliance is clear and imperative.

Ted Galen Carpenter
November 2018

1. Cold War to Holy War: The U.S.-Saudi Alliance

The Kingdom of Saudi Arabia's possession of the largest oil reserves in the world made it a highly valued U.S. Cold War ally. Senior policy planners, diplomatic officials, and defense and intelligence specialists deemed the industrial world's access to Saudi crude a vital national interest. That determination led to calls for establishing U.S. military predominance in the Persian Gulf. The means to secure U.S. ascendance involved acts of aggression, intervention, and subversion against prospective regional foes. Additionally, above the Arab kingdom's oil-rich sands lay the Islamic holy sites of Mecca and Medina. That powerful spiritual position in the Muslim world inspired top U.S. officials to forge a Christian-Islamic moral alliance with the Saudi royal family against pan-Arab socialists, secular nationalists, and godless Soviet communists.

For pragmatic reasons, Washington reluctantly accepted Riyadh's austere social dictates, many at odds with America's core foundational principles and basic standards of human rights. Saudi Arabia's absolute monarchy banned free speech, competitive elections, and political parties. It propagated a ferocious intolerance of Jews, prohibited the public mixing of unmarried women and men, and in a disturbing throwback to the Middle Ages, beheaded apostates, adulterers, drug traffickers, and homosexuals in public. The Saudi government enforced the public's observance not just to Islam, but to an ultra-conservative derivation called Wahhabism (Salafism by its adherents). Throughout the Islamic world, the kingdom exported its literalist interpretation of Islam, pouring its oil wealth into a network of religious schools, Islamic missionaries, and charitable organizations of global reach. Successive American administrations proved enthusiastic backers of Riyadh's influence, even as a viciously intolerant religious ideology rivaled oil as Saudi Arabia's chief export.

The U.S.-Saudi alliance's anti-nationalist, anti-communist crusade produced a decidedly mixed record. Reasonably encouraging short-term gains gave way to disastrously terrifying results in the long run. Few officials could have predicted the partnership's most grim and far-reaching consequences: the birth of al Qaeda, the spread of the radical Muslim Brotherhood, and the growth of a fanatical ideology that justified indiscriminate killing and mass murder. The U.S.-Saudi alliance, one of the world's most enduring, complex, and less publicized partnerships, not only extended U.S. security and political cover to an oppressive, reactionary theocracy, but also nurtured that theocracy's diffusion of malignant ideas and movements that continue to infect the world today.

Oil Diplomacy, Corporate Diplomacy

Before the Kingdom of Saudi Arabia evolved into the commercially sophisticated and oil-rich monarchy of today, its rickety fiefdom soared, collapsed, and reemerged through religious proselytizing and military conquest. That struggle for survival, rather than the desert kingdom's seeming intolerance for modernity, drove its alliance with the West. In mid-18th-century Najd, the Arabian Peninsula's central region, Islamic theologian Muhammad Ibn Abd al-Wahhab spearheaded a movement to expunge his religion of practices and innovations arising after Allah's revelations to the Prophet Mohammed in the 7th century.[1]

Abd al-Wahhab made defiance to authority punishable by death, while preaching the virtues of social harmony. He denounced usury, saint worship, and inattention to prayer, while instructing how to properly shake hands, embrace, and laugh, among other social and personal behaviors. After a local village chieftain expelled Abd al-Wahhab for his radical teachings, he fled to al-Diriya, a town on the outskirts of modern Riyadh, where he came under the protection of local emir Muhammad Ibn Al-Saud, the forefather of the Saudi royal family, the House of Saud.[2] In 1744, with Abd al-Wahhab's desire to spread his puritanical teachings and Al-Saud's need to subdue Bedouin tribes, they formed a religious-political alliance and expanded their geographic dominion by the sword of *jihad* (struggle for the faith of Islam). Their spiritual-warrior followers called themselves Unitarians (*muwahiddun*), but outsiders called them Wahhabists.

Over the centuries, that alliance seized, lost, and recaptured vast stretches of the Arabian Peninsula under the Turkicized Islam of

Ottoman rule. By the early 1920s, in a conquest that totaled 40,000 executions and 350,000 amputations, King Ibn Saud[3] and his estimated 50,000-strong religious army (*Ikhwan*) took al-Hejaz, the Red Sea emirate holding Islam's holiest cities of Mecca, toward which pious Muslims turn to pray, and Medina, burial site of the Prophet Muhammad. On September 23, 1932, after putting down revolts from his elite but unruly *Ikhwan* and consulting the region's tribal sheikhs and theologians, King Ibn Saud unified the state, with Wahhabism as its legal and constitutional basis.

The newly formed kingdom's messianic zeal failed to preclude its orientation toward the West. A key reason was that the West provided the capital-intensive tools and open markets necessary for Saudi Arabia to tap its oil wealth effectively. In May 1933, King Ibn Saud granted Standard Oil Company of California (Socal, later Chevron) an exclusive, 60-year concession to explore and extract his country's petroleum in return for a percentage of profits.[4] By 1938, the oil consortium later known as the Arabian-American Oil Company (Aramco)—comprised of Socal, Standard Oil Company of New Jersey (Standard Oil, later Exxon), Mobil, and Texaco—discovered vast petroleum deposits.

After 1941, when Saudi oil fields began pumping commercial quantities for export, the revenue eventually allowed Al Saud kings and crown princes, serving as top officials, provincial governors, and heads of ministerial agencies, to build their country into a centralized, administrative-bureaucratic state. The Saudis were zealous about protecting their national culture, even as they accepted foreign technology. For instance, the contract with Socal contained an "anti-imperial" clause, which prohibited company influence on Saudi policies.[5] Former U.S. Ambassador to Saudi Arabia Chas W. Freeman Jr. clarifies how the Saudis barred Euro-American intrusions:

> When Westerners finally gained access to the Kingdom of Saudi Arabia, it was under contract as 'hired help,' not as conquerors. Americans and Europeans were able to enter the Kingdom only so long as they evinced respect for Saudi religious and social tradition and accepted that any attempt to propagate Western religious, ideological, or secular values would result in summary punishment and/or deportation.[6]

To appease those in society who resisted an oil industry run by infidel expatriates, and modern innovations like planes, automobiles, telegraphs, and radios, the king consulted a body of religious scholars (*ulema*), who adjudicated disputes, issued official religious-legal rulings (*fatwas*), and ensured the observance of Wahhabism.[7]

To contest rival sheikhs and emirs in the Gulf, King Ibn Saud needed foreign assistance. The British Empire, which had colonies in Kuwait, Qatar, Bahrain, Oman, and the Indian subcontinent and protectorates over Iran, Iraq, and Anglo-Egyptian Sudan, helped Saudi Arabia seize al-Hejaz from the Hashemites, the future rulers of Iraq and Transjordan. But British imperial planners encroached on Ibn Saud's sphere of influence in the southern Arabian Peninsula and catapulted the Hashemites to the forefront of Arab leadership. The king began to consider America as the foreign power with which to align for his country's security.[8] Recalls former U.S. Ambassador to Saudi Arabia Parker T. Hart, one reason Ibn Saud gave for turning to America, "you are very far away!"[9]

By World War II, when Saudi territory provided the allies an air route for sending troops and supplies to the India-Burma Theater, oil company representatives and top U.S. officials urged President Franklin D. Roosevelt to expand that nascent cooperation to safeguard U.S. petroleum interests. James A. Moffett, a friend of Roosevelt's, a petroleum adviser to the White House, and acting in the interest of California-Arabian Standard Oil Company, advocated U.S. aid to Ibn Saud by stressing the king's dwindling resources and the specter of Britain monopolizing postwar oil concessions. W. S. S. Rodgers, the chairman of Texaco, circulated a memorandum to the U.S. Secretaries of War, Navy, and Interior, emphasizing Washington's long-term need for an abundant supply of petroleum.[10] Harold Ickes, petroleum administrator for war and secretary of the interior, insisted that oil was too vital a commodity to leave in private hands.[11]

In 1943, Roosevelt instructed Lend-Lease administrator and U.S. steel mogul Edward R. Stettinius Jr. to make the Saudi government eligible for wartime aid. Under Executive Order No. 8926, which laid the groundwork for a broader alliance and decades of U.S.-Middle East policy, Roosevelt's directive read succinctly: "I hereby find that the defense of Saudi Arabia is vital to the defense of the United States."[12]

On February 14, 1945, in one of history's most iconic moments, President Roosevelt met King Ibn Saud aboard the USS *Quincy* on the Great Bitter Lake in the Suez Canal. The countries date their "special relationship" to this personal meeting, but aside from discussing the question of Palestine, nobody knows if they talked about oil.[13] Afterward, the U.S. and Saudi foreign policy establishments entered a formal military alliance, and Washington pledged to protect Riyadh from prospective enemies in order to secure the industrial world's uninterrupted access to Saudi crude. State Department Near Eastern Affairs Division Chief Gordon Merriam called Saudi oil "a stupendous source of strategic power, and one of the greatest material prizes in world history."[14] That tacit oil-for-security partnership underpinned over half a century of sustained global economic growth. It also made U.S. energy and national security policies inextricably entwined.

More expansive policies with the kingdom began under Roosevelt's successor, President Harry S. Truman. His newly formed Central Intelligence Agency (CIA) determined in October 1947 that denying "a major, hostile, expansionist power" control of the Persian Gulf was as essential as maintaining, "access to the oil of the Persian Gulf area."[15] Equating access to oil with control of it, officials rationalized sheltering Saudi Arabia under the U.S. security umbrella. At U.S.-taxpayer expense the previous year, officials had helped the Saudis complete an enormous military and commercial airfield in Dhahran on the kingdom's eastern coast. The undersecretary of the navy believed that "the mere existence of an American military airfield at Dhahran would contribute to the preservation of the political integrity of Saudi Arabia and to the maintenance of our interest in the oil fields."[16]

Dhahran airbase not only placed Saudi Arabia's oil "in American hands," but also enabled the United States to deploy, base, and operate on Saudi soil for other international projects. Dhahran shortened America's route to the Pacific, as the only base under U.S. Army control between Libya and Pakistan. It also allowed refueling on long-haul air operations for the nuclear-armed, long-range bomber force, the Strategic Air Command. Saudi territory became a springboard for the projection of U.S. military power in and beyond the Persian Gulf. The Saudi connection improved America's "world-wide strategic position," wrote Secretary of Defense James Forrestal.[17]

With Saudi Arabia incorporated into America's globe-girdling series of military outposts, top U.S. decisionmakers and leading thinkers steered America's Middle East policy in a direction favorable to
oil interests. Many political leaders, academics, and federal and state
judges believed America's largest corporations could not act independent of social considerations. Corporations acted as "arms of the
state" and constituted forms of "private government."[18]

The Petroleum Reserves Corporation, a U.S.-government entity
tasked with acquiring petroleum outside the continental United
States, provided the California-based engineering company Bechtel
nearly $135 million to construct an oil pipeline for oil consortium
Aramco known as the Trans-Arabian Pipeline (Tapline). From the
Persian Gulf to the Eastern Mediterranean, Tapline would send oil
to markets in Western Europe for its postwar economic recovery.
Alas, President Shukri Quwatly of Syria refused Aramco the right
of way through his territory. Oil company executives began giving
Damascus ultimatums, upsetting King Ibn Saud's anti-imperialist
sensibilities.[19]

U.S. officials saw the refusal of Arab leaders to see things America's
way "as ample reason and justification for us to overthrow them—or
rather, to enable their own people to overthrow them," wrote Miles
Copeland, the CIA station chief in Damascus.[20] With the CIA's dis-
creet backing, Syrian Army Chief Husni al-Zaim—"the Americans'
boy," as Copeland put it—overthrew President Quwatly in March
1949.[21] Al-Zaim promptly completed several oil deals with U.S. and
British companies. By December, after Syrian army officers ousted
and executed al-Zaim, pro-American Army Colonel Adib Shishakli
restored Western influence. The State Department explained that
nothing would interfere with relations between Saudi Arabia and
Aramco because, "this relationship was the basis for the harmony
between this government and the Arabian government."[22] By December 1950, Tapline was complete.

Along with bringing the kingdom's massive energy resources
to Western markets, President Truman opened another facet of the
partnership in autumn 1950. In a letter to King Ibn Saud, Truman
called their countries "comrades in arms" opposing "the godless
forces of Communism . . . endeavoring to destroy freedom throughout the world." The following year, from the CIA's vantage point,
threats to Saudi royalists and other pro-Western regimes emerged

from both "Communist pressure" and "the anti-Western national-ism of Iran and the Arab world."[23] Officials hoped the Saudi king, as the guardian of the holy places of Islam, could rally Muslims be-hind America's anti-Communist cause and strengthen Washington's standing across the Islamic World. In a meeting with representatives from the CIA, State, and Defense, one official raised the idea of pro-moting King Ibn Saud as a "Moslem Billy Graham."[24] As the "head of the puritanical Wahhabi movement to restore the pure faith and practices of Islam"—wrote William A. Eddy, the U.S. consul general in Dhahran, in a June 1951 letter—the monarch was "the most repre-sentative and influential Muslim in the world today."[25]

That year, in addition to a mutual-defense-assistance pact supply-ing the kingdom with American weapons, permitting "show-the-flag" military visits, and stationing U.S. technical personnel on Saudi soil, Washington showed a genuine interest in forging a moral alli-ance with the kingdom. Eddy described the strategy as "the Chris-tian democratic West joining with the Muslim world in a common moral front against Communism." Although presidents Roosevelt and Truman laid the economic and security foundations of the part-nership, their successors would progressively expand the alliance's moral and ideological dimension.

Into the Vortex: The "Arab Cold War"

Amid its competition with Moscow, the White House worked with the House of Saud to influence Muslim public opinion. The Psychological Strategy Board, a Truman-era creation later renamed the Operations Coordinating Board, headed most of Washington's propaganda activities in the Islamic world. One of its programs, ad-opted by President Dwight D. Eisenhower but planned under his predecessor, stressed the pervading influence of faith on Arab think-ing. The board's psychological operations expert, Edward P. Lilly, wrote "The Religious Factor," a memorandum in early 1953 that called on Washington to use the power of religion more explicitly.[26] Beyond extending the short-term lease on Dhahran that June and pledging a U.S. Military and Training Mission to advise and assist the kingdom's military, U.S. officials devised a variety of ways to work with the Saudis and mold Muslim minds in support of anti-Soviet policies.[27]

Geopolitics makes for strange bedfellows, with Washington's psychological activities putting it in league with one of the 20th century's most influential pan-Islamist movements—the Muslim Brotherhood. Hassan al-Banna (1905–1949), the Egyptian schoolteacher and imam who founded the transnational religious society in 1928, studied under Muhammad Rashid Rida (1865–1935), a religious reformer influenced by Saudi-Wahhabist doctrine.[28] Al-Banna's anti-secular movement believed in defending Islam through political activism and advocated a system of Islamic republics spanning the global Muslim community (*ummah*). By the late 1940s, al-Banna had regular meetings with diplomat Hermann Eilts, who would later become the U.S. ambassador to Saudi Arabia.[29] Officials continued that ardent courting at the White House.

In the Oval Office on September 23, 1953, President Eisenhower met Said Ramadan, the Muslim Brotherhood's chief international organizer and the son-in-law of its founder.[30] Ramadan had established Muslim Brotherhood branches in Jerusalem, Damascus, and Amman, spreading the movement's dogmatic interpretation of Islam through schools, student groups, professional associations, and propaganda. For *El Musliman,* a monthly magazine of Islamic law and culture where Ramadan was editor-in-chief, subscribers ranged "from Tunisia to Indonesia," gushed U.S. Ambassador to Egypt Jefferson Caffery. Ramadan later offered to distribute *Arabic Review,* run by a CIA front organization in Munich, throughout the Arabic speaking world.[31]

The U.S. Library of Congress, Princeton University, and the International Information Administration at the State Department hosted a 10-day colloquium that brought Ramadan and over 50 other leading Islamic intellectuals to Washington. As U.S. officials stated, the colloquium aimed at giving "impetus and direction . . . to the Renaissance movement within Islam itself" and furthering "good will and mutual understanding between Islamic peoples and the United States."[32] Oil consortium Aramco defrayed some of the travel costs for Muslim Brotherhood members to attend.[33]

Although officials hoped to rally the Muslim Brotherhood against communism, another fear that America's North Atlantic Treaty Organization (NATO) allies expressed emanated from "rising Arab nationalism, fanned by extremists in the Arab states." As in Asia, Latin America, and elsewhere around the world, the Middle East's "anti-

imperialist" movements unnerved U.S. officials, who viewed such uprisings as fertile ground for Soviet-inspired communism. [34] Indeed, a
nationalist uprising in Egypt, the Arab world's most populous state,
birthed a secular, nationalist regime headed by Colonel Gamal Abdel
Nasser, who eventually became Saudi Arabia's most pressing security
threat and Washington's biggest headache in the Near East.

The charismatic Nasser rode a wave of populist sentiment to
expel Britain's colonial presence. After King Ibn Saud's death in
November 1953, his profligate heir, King Saud,[35] aligned with Nasser.
The Saudi monarch, guided primarily by Arab geopolitics, channeled money from U.S. oil companies to sponsor Nasser's propaganda campaigns against Bahrain and rival Hashemites in Iraq and
Jordan.[36] As for Washington, the CIA initially helped propel Nasser
to power in the hope of harnessing his sway over the Arab masses.
That strategy backfired quickly when he publicly ridiculed U.S.-
sponsored regional security arrangements like the 1955 Baghdad
Pact, which comprised Britain, Turkey, Iraq, Iran, and Pakistan. U.S.
officials would not only come to shun Arab secularists like Nasser,
but also to embrace the Saudis, the Muslim Brotherhood, and other
conservative monarchs and extreme religious movements.

No Jews Allowed

Straining otherwise solid U.S.-Saudi relations were controversies
over Israel, or more specifically, Saudi Arabia's extreme hostility not
only to Israel but to Jews generally. That hostility split U.S.–Middle
East policy into separate pro-Israel and pro-Arab camps. After World
War II and the tragedy of the Holocaust, many Americans deeply
sympathized with the plight of European Jewry. Pro-Israel American gentiles admired the Jewish people's quest for statehood and
Evangelical Christians supported Jewish migration to Palestine as
a fulfillment of Biblical prophecy.[37] As early as 1944, the Republican
and Democratic Parties adopted pro-Zionist planks. Accordingly, the
American people and their elected officials supported the United Nations (UN) partition of Palestine into separate Jewish and Arab states.

In sharp contrast, America's diplomatic, intelligence, and defense
communities did not. They strongly advised against U.S. support
for Palestine's partition.[38] Senior policy planners concluded that the
suffering of Palestinian refugees, and the impression that America

protected Zionists, would encourage Arab states to retaliate by either limiting Western access to the region or cultivating ties with the Soviets. The Joint Chiefs of Staff urged no action occur that would orient Arabs away from the West.[39] But as a result of Washington's sponsorship of the UN partition plan of November 1947, a report by the State Department's policy planning staff remarked, "U.S. prestige in the Moslem world has suffered a severe blow and U.S. strategic interests in the Mediterranean and the Near East have been seriously prejudiced."[40]

The divergence between American public sympathies and elite strategic consensus created a duality in the shaping of U.S. statecraft in the Middle East broadly, and toward Saudi Arabia specifically. Riyadh's anti-Israel policies punctuated the partnership with a pattern of highly public controversies. For instance, provisions in the Dhahran airbase lease agreement allowed the Arab kingdom to deny transit to Israelis, people of Jewish descent, and visitors with an Israeli-stamped passport. Those provisions affected diplomats, service members, reporters, lawmakers, business leaders, and tourists. Although U.S. officials never formally approved such discriminatory practices, they submitted detailed lists of names, identities, and religious affiliations of U.S. personnel assigned to the kingdom—enabling Riyadh to exclude whomever it wished. President Eisenhower reflected on the matter years later:

> It cannot be denied that many of the Arab actions, irritating to the Israelis, seemed to be inspired by nothing more than hatred of every Jew, merely because he was a Jew. In our government's negotiations for landing rights in Saudi Arabia for American military personnel, one of the conditions imposed by the Saudi government was that no Jew would be allowed on the field.[41]

In early February 1956, during negotiations for America's renewal of Dhahran's lease, Secretary of State John Foster Dulles told the Senate Foreign Relations Committee, "We don't like to acquiesce, but we have to recognize that Saudi Arabia is an ally."[42] Acquiesce administration leaders did, leading to an anemic Senate resolution in July implicitly criticizing Riyadh's practices. That resolution stated that any attempt by foreign nations to discriminate against American citizens based on their individual religious affiliations was generally "inconsistent with our principles."[43]

That feeble condemnation tempered neither the American public's lingering animosities toward the Saudi regime, nor the Saudi regime's hatred of Israel. When UN Secretary General Dag Hammarskjöld invited King Saud to address the General Assembly the following year, New York City Mayor Robert Wagner announced he would not turn on a single traffic light to help "this monkey."[44] Additionally, King Saud derided as a provocation against Muslims when an Israeli company, chartering a U.S. tanker, proceeded through the international waterway Gulf of Aqaba, which he considered an Arab possession.[45]

To some extent, Saudi intolerance regarding Israel (and Jewish people in any locale) reflected its generally illiberal internal disposition. The regime enforced its rigid Wahhabi religious precepts and social behaviors through government-subsided morality police, the *mutawwa'in,* known by their Orwellian title, Committee for the Propagation of Virtue and the Prevention of Vice. These semiautonomous, ultra-conservative zealots inflicted daily human suffering and misery.[46] They harassed, intimidated, abused, and detained citizens and foreigners alike. Yet, for the White House, the oil-for-security partnership trumped American pluralism and basic human rights. Even as the United States professed to stand by the highest of principles, it applied a very different standard to suit its instrumental objectives in countering Arab nationalists. When it came to the Saudi totalitarian theocracy's systemic repression, both U.S. rhetoric and practices regarding human rights took a back seat.

Masters vs. Subjects

Eisenhower administration officials, like Truman's, also suggested grooming the Saudi king as an Arab leader and a religious rival to Nasser. A CIA survey of Radio Cairo's reception discovered that all parts of the Arab world, from Iraq to Morocco, heard Nasser's propaganda promoting the mythology of pan-Arab nationalism through his popular broadcast "Voice of the Arabs."[47] By March 1956, President Eisenhower grew concerned over what he called "the growing ambition of Nasser" and "his belief that he can emerge as the true leader of the entire Arab World."[48] Regardless of Nasser's motives, U.S. officials believed he abetted Soviet penetration of the Near East. In covert plan Project Omega, senior CIA officials and representatives from State and Defense sought to reduce Nasser's influence, counter Soviet arms deals to Arab states, and strengthen pro-Western regimes in Jordan, Lebanon, and Saudi Arabia. Meanwhile, Washington and London worked to subvert nationalists who largely resisted cooperation, coercion, and control by the West.[49] From Iran and Egypt to Syria and Jordan, Washington and London utilized political assassinations, violent covert action, and other cloak-and-dagger operations to bend to Western interests the region's organic process of political emancipation.

The Anglo-American allies differed, however, over how to counter Nasser and the Arab secular nationalists. Those diverging views came to a head with the Suez Canal Crisis, a flashpoint that cemented Washington's long-standing commitment to the region's conservative, oil-rich monarchies. The crisis also brought into sharper focus the so-called "Arab Cold War," the intraregional divide that pitted Saudi Arabia and other Western-backed guardians of the status quo against Egypt and other Soviet-backed secular-nationalist regimes.[50]

In late October 1956, Israel invaded Egypt, and that move was followed in early November with bombings from Britain and France. President Eisenhower—shocked by allied hostilities he thought reeked of 19th-century imperialism—promptly pulled support for the British pound, refused oil deliveries to France, and threatened to back UN sanctions against Israel. The Suez crisis devolved into a political catastrophe and irrevocably damaged the image of Britain and France as world powers. In response to the willingness to confront Israel and Washington's own NATO allies, America's status across the region skyrocketed.[51]

For merely withstanding the Israeli-British-French-"Zionist-Crusader" invasion, Nasser ascended to regional and global prominence. In the decade after Suez, pro-Nasserite parties sprouted in Lebanon, Syria, Jordan, Iraq, and Arab states in the Gulf, as his pan-Arab nationalism and Arab socialism emerged as the mainstream of Arab geopolitics for nearly a generation.[52] Nasser preached defiance to the forces that attacked him in Suez and denounced as subservient puppets, reactionary rulers, and tools of "imperialist interests" neighboring states that remained tied to them. Most importantly, the fiery-tongued ruler poured out his scorn on Saudi Arabia. He castigated the kingdom as "occupied" by foreign troops, called Dhahran airbase a concession to American imperialism, and admonished the royal family for hoarding oil wealth from its destitute Arab neighbors.[53]

With Nasser's blend of anti-Western and anti-royalist attitudes appealing to Arabs living under pro-Western monarchs, the Eisenhower administration decided to fill the void left by its defeated NATO allies. On January 5, 1957, in the annual State of the Union Address, President Eisenhower requested the authority to send America's military forces to repel "overt armed aggression from any country controlled by International Communism" in the Middle East. As he explained, that region "contains about two thirds of the presently known oil deposits of the world." Many nations depended on that petroleum.[54]

King Saud, during his first visit to Washington that month, threw his full support behind Eisenhower. They signed a five-year renewal of America's lease at Dhahran airbase, and King Saud pursued rapprochement with Iraq and Jordan. He signed a communiqué on the need to stand against all "communist activities" and launched a propaganda campaign against "world communism." Washington agreed to pay, train, and expand Saudi Arabia's army, provide the kingdom with $25 million in loans, and supply its military with ground vehicles, aircraft, and naval equipment.[55] On March 9, Congress passed a joint resolution that became known as the Eisenhower Doctrine. It gave the executive branch the authority to wage war in defense of America's Middle East allies. Meanwhile, as America emerged as the primary source of the kingdom's security, U.S. officials worked more aggressively with Islamic leaders to oppose what President Eisenhower described as "the implacable enmity of godless communism."[56]

Amid the Red scare that gripped Washington, Hollywood, and much of America during this time, high-ranking officials regarded such measures as appropriate, particularly given the few Muslim communities Washington could tap into compared to the estimated 30 million Muslim citizens living under the Bolsheviks. As the head of a Western, predominantly Christian nation, Eisenhower authorized half a million dollars to refurbish Mecca.[57] An Ad Hoc Working Group on Islam, under the propaganda activities of the Operations

Coordinating Board, developed an "Outline Plan of Operations" calling for Washington to side with "reform" groups like the Muslim Brotherhood. "The President said he thought we should do everything possible to stress the 'holy war' aspect," detailed the memorandum of a meeting with Eisenhower, the Joint Chiefs of Staff, and CIA covert operations czar Frank Wisner. According to a later estimate by CIA Director William Colby, up to half of the CIA's budget at the time went to propaganda, political action, and paramilitary operations.[58] Additionally, of the more than $100 million the spy agency spent on anti-Nasser operations, some ended up in the hands of the Muslim Brotherhood, according to defense intelligence officer, CIA adviser, and military attaché Wilbur Crane Eveland.[59]

In its quest to counter Arab states allegedly "manipulated by International Communism," Washington embraced the misbegotten inheritance of European imperialism, placing a bulls-eye on the kingdom's enemies and eventually exacerbating the nationalist sentiments it sought to contest. After numerous botched U.S. and British coups against Arab nationalists in Cairo and Damascus, the Egyptian and Syrian governments merged into the United Arab Republic (UAR) in February 1958. In response, second cousins King Faisal II of Iraq and King Hussein of Jordan formed the Arab Federation, alternatively known as the Arab Union. That alliance proved short-lived.

In what would prove to be a prescient statement of the post-9/11 world, U.S. officials at the time, including State Department Near Eastern Affairs Director Stuart W. Rockwell, supported Faisal, but conceded, "there are disadvantages to a close identification of the United States with the regional and internal political policies of the Arab Union and its component governments."[60] That appraisal, albeit accurate, still amounted to a serious underestimation of the complex environment in which America operated. U.S. foreign policy planners were not chiefly responsible for the Middle East's severe political and socioeconomic dysfunction; however, Washington's generous support to the region's repressive tyrants constituted an artificial prop that kept unrepresentative leaders in power. Arab subjects who opposed Western-backed autocrats thus came to view the West as a major impediment to their economic development and political self-determination. For decades, that prominent feature of America's engagement with the Middle East would feed evergrowing, increasingly rabid anti-American sentiment.

Concerns over petroleum supplies and communist machinations, however, precluded a change of course. The intractability of policy resigned even the most cognizant officials to callous indifference. Backing treacherous tyrants naturally muted calls for reform and standing for America's higher purpose. "Popularity," wrote Rockwell, "in itself in this part of the world is not necessarily an essential element for the survival of a government." That attitude, intuitively appealing to some experts, implied that people of the region willingly submitted to undisputed rulers—that somehow, capitulation to despotism was part of Arab self-identity. That monolithic view rationalized abusive practices and rigid social and political structures. It also allowed U.S. officials to blame dynamics beyond their control, exempting their official support for dictators who deprived their subjects of Western-style freedoms.

On July 14, 1958, after years of the CIA blanketing Iraq with pro-Western propaganda and bribing its "mildly pinkish" leaders to accept anti-Soviet alliances, a band of pro-Nasserite army officers seized control in Baghdad. They acquired documents confirming the previous leadership's schemes for U.S. subversion against Syria, the Baghdad Pact's secret military plans, and at least $45 million worth of U.S. military assistance. President Eisenhower relayed the next day that many of the deposed monarchy's leading personalities "were beaten to death or hanged and their bodies dragged through the streets."[61] Iraq's brutal revolution and the collapse of the Baghdad Pact's key regional power sent shockwaves across the region and alarmed the Saudi royal family.

"What is the use of all these pacts?" exclaimed King Saud's personal emissary on America's failure to intervene.[62] CIA Director Allen Dulles stopped short of saying the Soviets would get directly involved, but nevertheless cast Iraq's military coup in terms of the prevailing domino theory, warning that the events in Baghdad threatened to doom pro-West governments in Lebanon, Jordan, and Saudi Arabia. British soldiers deployed to Jordan to save that country's monarch. Eisenhower dispatched 6,000 marines and 2,500 army personnel to secure the territorial integrity and political independence of Lebanon in Operation Blue Bat within 72 hours of Baghdad's fall.[63]

Whatever the cause of Lebanon's unrest, the injection of Western forces provoked anger in much of the Arab world. "The United States seems to have become anathema to the region," President

Eisenhower observed on July 23. Though he wanted to get "to the point where the Arabs will not be hostile to us," Western actions, especially the military interventions, vindicated that hostility.[64] U.S. officials pledged to protect repressive regimes, like Saudi Arabia, and absorb the military and political risks of doing so. Additionally, waning European colonialism and the growth of nationalist uprisings against it put American leaders in an anomalous position. Indeed, Eisenhower remained sensitive to the impression that America stood as a beacon of hope even to anti-colonial, Third World Elements:

> Among all the powerful nations of the world the United States is the only one with a tradition of anti-colonialism. . . . The standing of the United States as the most powerful of the anti-colonial powers is an asset of incalculable value to the Free World.[65]

U.S. officials may have supported self-determination in principle, but global strategy and tactics pushed against such abstractions. While America's values accorded with the postcolonial struggle for freedom, tough questions surrounded how best to achieve that goal. After all, despite Eisenhower's firm stance during Suez—or perhaps even because of it—Nasser's sway over the Arab masses made him increasingly resistant to Western appeals for moderation.

Weeks after America's intervention in Lebanon, the National Security Council Planning Board advised that "We must adjust to the tide of Arab nationalism, and must do so before the hotheads get control in every country."[66] Eisenhower's successor adopted that approach, but unnecessarily ensnared his administration in another intra-Arab conflict.

The Arab Cold War Heats Up

As with India's Jawaharlal Nehru, Ghana's Kwame Nkrumah, and other Third World neutrals, President John F. Kennedy wanted "a reasonably balanced policy" with Nasser to counterbalance communism.[67] His olive branch cast a noticeable chill over Washington's relations with Riyadh, especially as Kennedy championed in his May 1961 message to Congress the importance of social progress and "economic reform and development," chiding foreign governments unwilling to change with the times.[68] He argued that U.S. arms and aid alone could not stabilize reactionary regimes, an oblique reference to Saudi Arabia, which still had a thriving slave trade and remained far from social progress. That month, Riyadh informed Washington that it would terminate the lease on Dhahran upon its expiration the following June.[69] Relations between President Kennedy and King Saud also grew chilly after they exchanged personal slights in written correspondence. But as Washington's ties with Cairo improved, including the distribution of U.S. agricultural commodities to Egypt, the toppling of another conservative Arab monarch derailed Kennedy's fragile détente with Nasser and swung U.S. support back to Saudi Arabia.

On September 19, 1962, in Sana'a, Yemen's capital, pro-Nasserite military officers overthrew the newly installed imam and established the Yemen Arab Republic. The fourth military coup d'état in the Arab world—Egypt, Syria, Iraq, and now Yemen—horrified the Saudis. Yemen's closed society bordered Saudi Arabia's to the south, and its religious, yet corrupted, feudal royal family also ruled a scattered population susceptible to Arab nationalist propaganda. Riyadh pumped money and weapons to Yemen's deposed royalists and tribal sheikhs, and by October, Cairo dispatched a contingent of 18,000 troops to back the country's new revolutionary regime.[70]

"I don't even know where it is," Kennedy reportedly blurted out upon hearing of Yemen's tumult.[71] Regardless, the proxy conflict spurred intense debate in Washington over whether to recognize the military regime. The CIA and the Arabian Peninsula affairs chief reported that Yemen's power struggle was neither conducive to communist influence nor worthy of U.S. involvement.[72] But after Yemen-based UAR air units attacked the kingdom in November, Kennedy authorized brief military aircraft demonstrations over Riyadh and Jeddah. By then, White House National Security Council aide Robert Komer and Secretary of State Dean Rusk argued that delaying recognition risked extending social revolution into Saudi Arabia.[73] Some specialists in the Near East Bureau believed recognition would encourage Nasser to extract his forces and show that America sided with the nationalist "wave of the future."[74] When the Saudi-backed royalists looked destined for defeat, the United States formally recognized Yemen's pro-Nasserite government on December 19, 1962. Rather than abstain from political interference until the dust settled,

25

Washington recognized a wobbly military regime backed by a nationalist Arab state that had attacked a U.S. ally and publicly called for its overthrow. In the end, the gesture flopped.

President Kennedy, quite rightly, had separated Arab nationalism from external communist control, a volte-face from his predecessors. Communism never was monolithic, nor were its imagined subsidiaries in the Third World. Nevertheless, the administration's recognition of Yemen revealed an attractive temptation that regularly entraps U.S. policymakers: the urge to address complex problems without a constructive way to resolve them. Despite Nasser's promises to withdraw his expeditionary forces, Washington had limited means of stopping further escalation in the absence of securing a formal disengagement agreement from the parties.[75] Officials also left unanswered precisely how Yemen's recognition would give the "Arab Cold War's" two main belligerents a face-saving exit from their proxy conflict, as domestic power struggles guided their response to the crisis.

Wooing Nasser assumed he would readily jettison his pan-Arab revolution to deepen relations with Washington. That assumption proved unfounded. Meanwhile, there was substantial turmoil within the Saudi royal family. A month before Yemen's coup, Prince Talal[76] openly sided with Nasser and defected to Cairo. His brother, half-brother, cousin, and others joined him, advocating a "Free Princes" reformist movement, a constitutional monarchy, and expanded civil rights. The embarrassment compromised the kingdom's legitimacy. When King Faisal[77] took the reins of power in November 1964, his fight against secular nationalists won him support among Saudi religious elites.[78]

Kennedy went from playing peacemaker to throwing fuel on the inferno by tacitly approving Saudi Arabia's funding of Yemen's Muslim Brotherhood against UAR forces. The CIA also arranged for the approval of a passport for the Muslim Brotherhood's globe-trotting ambassador, Said Ramadan, who a year before Yemen's coup founded the Islamic Center of Geneva.[79] The think tank, funded largely by the Saudis, spread the brethren's puritanical brand of Islam across Western Europe. Whether Ramadan received CIA funding is difficult to determine, but nonetheless probable: Swiss authorities later described Ramadan as an "information agent" of Britain and America, and German intelligence documents claimed America financed Ramadan's expenditures.[80]

In addition to international Muslim Brotherhood branches and a mosque in Munich he helped raise money to build, Ramadan helped found the Muslim World League in May 1962. The Mecca-based, nongovernmental organization, in the words of one scholar, aimed to "'Wahhabize' Islam world wide."[81] It sponsored conferences and symposia, published books and papers, and funded an international network of religious charities. With 99 percent of its funding coming from the Saudi state, along with its secretary-generals becoming ministers in the Saudi government and senior religious figures comprising its Constituent Council, the organization acted as a veritable extension of Saudi national policy.[82] Even as the royal family busily spread its puritanical religious doctrine, President Kennedy intended to display another show of military force in defense of the kingdom. But his effort to soothe Saudi anxieties triggered controversy in Washington.

"Personnel of Jewish faith or Jewish extraction will not be selected," began an April 1963 U.S. Air Force operations manual's planned personnel section.[83] The Pentagon later removed the sentence, but Rep. Emanuel Celler (D-NY) disclosed in a June 10th radio interview that Jewish-American personnel might deploy to the kingdom.[84] The Saudi government demanded that Kennedy rebuke the congressman. Assistant Secretary of State Phillips Talbot told U.S. Ambassador Peter Hart that with Martin Luther King Jr. sitting in a Birmingham jail cell and black children being blasted with water cannon, the prospect of Washington defending Saudi discrimination was "totally out of the question."[85] Instead, Washington provided Riyadh political cover, claiming Saudi anti-Semitism had never arisen.

U.S. officials refused to challenge its ally's rampant anti-Semitism, both out of respect for Saudi sovereignty and to satisfy perceived U.S. national interests. But Riyadh's internal disposition precluded reciprocity—it insisted foreigners not interfere in the kingdom's social biases, while demanding that the policies of allied countries bend to Saudi norms. Saudi practices and Riyadh's diplomatic double standard did not merely raise uncomfortable questions, they obstructed a course of action intended to protect the country. At the same time, Washington's defense of the anti-Semitic kingdom risked aerial combat with the Egyptian air force.[86]

Two days after Celler's interview, Kennedy authorized Operation Hard Surface, which provided a squadron of eight tactical fighter aircraft, one transport aircraft, 560 support personnel, and over 800 tons of equipment to the kingdom.[87] General Maxwell Taylor, chairman of the Joint Chiefs of Staff, warned that Hard Surface put U.S. pilots in the difficult position of either responding militarily if engaged or risking America's military credibility. Air Force Chief of Staff Curtis Lemay warned that U.S. aircraft would be sitting ducks. Some at the Pentagon joked that Saudi pilots were too busy defecting to Egypt and called the operation a token defense. By October, Kennedy reduced his military bluff in the Eastern Mediterranean and the Red Sea to two tactical fighter wings, a second Sixth Fleet carrier task force, and a squadron of aging B-47 bombers.[88]

Overall, the conflicts and nationalist uprisings in Yemen, Lebanon, and elsewhere emerged from localized tensions, not broader U.S.-Soviet antagonisms. Kennedy said as much just weeks before his assassination in Dallas. In a speech before the Protestant Council of New York City, he described the dozen or more Third World proxy conflicts, including between "two Arab states over Yemen," as follows:

> The parties to these disputes have more in common
> ethnically and ideologically than do the Soviet Union
> and the United States. . . . In almost every case, their
> continuing conflict invites outside intervention and
> threatens worldwide escalation—yet the major pow-
> ers are hard put to limit events in these areas.[89]

Nasser eventually took to calling Yemen's civil war, "my Vietnam,"[90] and, by the end of the decade, Riyadh and Cairo would put aside their many differences.

The Middle East Remade

Top officials often referred to King Faisal as a moderate—a seductive yet myopic judgment. He may have maintained a pro-American stance and reformed his kingdom's administrative bodies, but the modernizer also intensified missionary preaching and Islamic call (*da'wa*), most profoundly in the Saudi higher-education system.

Despite the kingdom's prohibitions on political parties, it granted thousands of Muslim Brotherhood members sanctuary after Cairo banned the movement in 1948, and Nasser drove it underground and into exile following its attempt on his life in 1954. Brotherhood members fled to Jordan, Lebanon, Syria, and especially Saudi Arabia. Indeed, Saudi Arabia emerged as the brethren's chief operating base and principal financial backer.[91]

By the early 1960s, Nasser altered curriculum at al-Azhar, Cairo's thousand-year-old center of Islamic learning, to compete with Saudi Arabia's centrality in Islam. In response, King Faisal founded and lavishly funded the Islamic University of Medina in 1961 and King Abdulaziz University in 1967 and threw open their doors to Egyptian Islamic scholars. Descendants of Wahhabism's founder, the Al ash-Shaikh, controlled the Ministry of Education and its network of Islamic universities. But as they intermarried with members of the Al Saud, some adopted the Muslim Brotherhood's teachings, melding Wahhabism's austere theology with the Brotherhood's political activism. From that cross-fertilization sprung the precursor of Salafi pan-Islamism (*Salafiyya*), the radical, revivalist movement that germinated al Qaeda.[92]

Many university students studied curriculum tied closely to Islamic laws and teachings, including the work of the prolific anti-American writer and influential Egyptian Muslim Brotherhood member, Sayyid Qutb.[93] Rather than jihad understood as one's internal struggle, Qutb endorsed militant jihad, proclaiming that only from the Quran could true Muslims derive principles of government, politics, and economics. He claimed those professing otherwise were afflicted with a barbarous ignorance more insidious than humanity's state before Islam. Sheikh Abdel Aziz bin Baz, one of the kingdom's leading religious authorities, served as vice president and later president of the Islamic University of Medina. Despite medieval Islam's early contributions to celestial astronomy, Aziz bin Baz proclaimed the world was flat, and the Sun orbited the Earth.

Like Qutb, bin Baz condemned those who did not share his worldview as guilty of "falsehood toward God, the Koran, and the Prophet."[94] The kingdom later appointed the blind sheikh to be president of the Directorate of Religious Research, Missionary Activities, and Guidance, a permanent committee that oversaw the contents of religious sermons and was relied upon by many Muslims around the world for clerical legal rulings. These teachings spread in and beyond the Middle East; for instance, at the Islamic University of Medina, non-Saudis comprised 85 percent of the student body.[95] For some in society, travel abroad and exposure to foreign entertainment increased their desire for modern social transformation. For others, however, religious indoctrination bolstered their conservative Wahhabi predilections. Worldly and insular types alike began questioning concepts of life and the royal family's legitimacy (see chapter 13).[96] The significance of such trends failed to register in Washington.

Many top U.S. decisionmakers, diplomats, and defense and intelligence officials endorsed King Faisal's pan-Islamic efforts. The CIA encouraged Faisal's brother-in-law and intelligence chief, Kamal Adham—who had built a network of Islamist agents across the Arab world—to spend millions on the Muslim Brotherhood.[97] "We thought of Islam as a counterweight to communism," said Arabian Peninsula Affairs Chief Talcott Seelye, adding "we saw it as a moderate force, and a positive one."[98]

One CIA officer described the Mecca-based Muslim World League religious charity as "kind of a 'Vatican'-type organism."[99] That assertion was troubling. The Vatican had stopped denouncing pluralism and democracy as early as the 19th century. More important, in the absence of anti-clerical reaction in Islamic society, insofar as an ordered clergy existed, U.S. officials were making poor analogies and drawing erroneous conclusions. One Saudi-based British diplomat reported on the views of Washington and London:

> I take the relaxed view of Faisal's activities. . . . The American Embassy here, with whom we have discussed the subject at several levels, share this view. That is to say that the concept of Islam as an aggressive force has completely disappeared except among some older Saudis.[100]

That Anglo-American attitude grievously underestimated the political and ideological contagion they were helping disseminate.

Impact of the Six Day War of 1967 on U.S.-Saudi Ties

"Our relations with Saudi Arabia have been long, close, and cordial," affirmed President Lyndon Johnson during a meeting with King Faisal at the White House in June 1966. "As the venerable Arabic saying has it, 'Our house is your house.'"[101] Johnson continued his predecessors' commitment to the conservative, oil-rich monarchy. The British and U.S. governments signed an air defense program to fortify Saudi armed forces, including a $400 million initiative to build Saudi bases and $100 million for trucks and military transport vehicles.[102] But Johnson's generous accolades accompanied another public diplomacy embarrassment.

"Unfortunately," King Faisal replied when asked about U.S. companies doing business with Israel, "Jews support Israel and we consider those who provide assistance to our enemies as our own enemies."[103] New York Governor Nelson Rockefeller and New York City Mayor John V. Lindsay promptly canceled their scheduled engagements with the monarch. Faisal's vulgar recriminations were nothing new, but that bigotry was not frivolous. Although Johnson and other presidents believed the Soviets carried influence in the Middle East by exploiting regional tensions, former National Security Council member William B. Quandt explains that, in Faisal's view, U.S. support for Israel played into nationalist and communist hands, making the region more dangerous for the Saudis and other status quo forces.[104]

Raised by his maternal grandfather, a leading religious scholar and grandson of the founder of the puritanical Wahhabist movement, King Faisal expressed his frustration with Israel and Jews openly. He labeled communists and Jews as Islam's main enemies and charged that they were secretly allied to conquer the world. He even distributed copies of *The Protocols of the Elders of Zion,* a notorious, bogus, conspiratorial tract about a Jewish plot for global domination. Faisal called Marxism "a subversive creed originated by a vile Jew," and blamed Zionists for fomenting Palestinian terrorism.[105] Years later, Saudi Arabia strongly, and successfully, pushed for a UN General Assembly vote that equated Zionism with racism and the South African apartheid system. Faisal even described U.S.-Israel relations as a Zionist scheme to weaken Arab-American ties and undermine their Islamic-Christian struggle against communism.[106]

The kingdom's fervent opposition to Israel opened the U.S.-Saudi alliance's first significant breach. Shortly after the Arab League created the Palestine Liberation Organization (PLO) in 1964, the group splintered. Palestinian guerillas (*fedayeen*) launched raids against Israel from positions in Jordan, Lebanon, and the Gaza Strip (under Egyptian administration since 1949), and in retaliation, Israel inflicted heavy military punishment on Jordan in November 1966 and Syria in April 1967.[107] In a provocative attempt to burnish his nationalist image tarnished in Yemen and elsewhere, in May 1967, Nasser evicted UN military forces stationed on the Sinai since the Suez Crisis, moved his troops to Israel's southern border, and closed the Straits of Tiran to Israeli shipping. President Johnson condemned the blockade as illegal and urged Nasser to rescind it.[108]

Nevertheless, the conflict in Vietnam consumed the Johnson administration's attention and sorely shorthanded its foreign policy team. The Middle East post at the Policy Planning Council remained vacant between late 1966 and early 1967. The office of assistant secretary of state at the Near East Bureau stayed empty from November 1966 until April 1967. And Johnson's National Security Council rotated through three different Middle East directors between April 1966 and June 1967.

What Washington may have failed to fully appreciate was the extent to which the question of Palestine transcended intraregional differences and cemented Arab unity. On May 20, when asked by Aramco's vice president why the Saudi kingdom would object to Washington standing up to Nasser, Saudi Minister of Petroleum and Mineral Resources Ahmed Zaki Yamani replied, "We are all Arabs. Your government would be foolish if it does not keep out."[109] Shortly thereafter, Jordan and Iraq entered a military alliance with the UAR, and Syria, and Lebanon, Kuwait, and Saudi Arabia activated their armed forces.

On June 5, 1967, with the Egyptian, Syrian, and Jordanian armies poised on its borders, Israel launched a preemptive attack on all three. Within hours, it devastated Egypt's entire air force, along with Jordan's and half of Syria's. Iraq, Syria, Yemen, Algeria, Mauritania, and Sudan severed diplomatic relations with Washington and London after Nasser claimed falsely over Radio Cairo that they had provided Israel air support. In Dhahran, rioters stoned the U.S. Consulate, assaulted American citizens, and attacked Western vehicles, homes, and offices.[110] Following Kuwait, Iraq, Libya, and Algeria, on June 7, Saudi Arabia banned petroleum shipments to America and Britain. For the Saudis, solidarity came at a high price. The flow of Arab petroleum plummeted 60 percent within days. America, Venezuela, Iran, and Indonesia, though, increased their oil production and replaced the missing imports. Mecca Radio described the lost revenue as, "no less serious than Arab territorial and human losses in the war with Israel."[111]

After six days, Israel vanquished its Arab adversaries and thereby radically reshaped the modern Middle East. Israeli forces captured the Golan Heights from Syria, the West Bank and East Jerusalem from Jordan, and the Sinai Peninsula and Gaza Strip from Egypt. And—although rarely mentioned—Saudi Arabia's Tiran and Sanafir Islands fell to Israel.[112] Israel had dealt a psychological deathblow to the myth of pan-Arab strength. At the Arab League's August 1967 summit in Khartoum, Sudan, member states pledged no recognition of Israel, no peace, and no direct negotiations.[113] The Six Day War would also become the catalyst for Washington's expansive diplomatic involvement in the Arab-Israeli dispute. After the Jewish state defeated the Soviet Union's Arab clients, the U.S.-Israel patron-client partnership fully bloomed. Accordingly, America's image across the region plummeted, while Soviet prestige soared.[114]

Following Egypt's humiliating defeat, Saudi Arabia, albeit by default, emerged from the "Arab Cold War" victorious. As the strongest and most populous Arab state, Egypt had borne the brunt of the human, economic, and political costs of collective Arab wars against Israel. Cairo sought to restrain its ambitious foreign policy, and Riyadh eagerly filled the void. At Khartoum, Faisal and Nasser signed a peace settlement on Yemen, and the kingdom provided financial assistance to Cairo's economically ailing regime. Meanwhile, the region's religious conservatives and hard-line Islamists both blamed secular nationalism and the influence of Western ideologies for the Arab loss.

Perhaps most significant, Saudi Arabia, as the chief defender of Islam, broadened the pan-Arab struggle against Israel into a pan-Islamic one. He called for reclaiming East Jerusalem, and hence, al-Aqsa Mosque, Islam's third-holiest site, back from the Jewish state. On September 25, 1969, in Rabat, Morocco's capital, he convened delegations from 25 countries to establish the Organization of the

Islamic Conference, which advocated for the "struggle" in Palestine. After Nasser succumbed to a fatal heart attack in September 1970, Faisal increased his pan-Islamist efforts and used aid and loans to amplify the kingdom's influence. At the March 1972 Islamic summit in Jeddah, 31 countries agreed to a fund "for the holy war" against Israel and to support Palestinian guerillas.

The Saudi role regarding Palestine became increasingly prominent—and cynical. Weeks after the Six Day War, King Faisal explained to U.S. Ambassador Hermann Eilts during a meeting in Jeddah, "You are dealing with irrational people." Faisal said that Washington seemed unable to grasp what he called the Arab "mob psychology" prevalent among the region's "crazy people." Faisal and other pro-Western monarchs, he insisted, found themselves in a "bad spot," lacking anything they could identify "to show genuine [U.S. government] concern for Arab interests."[115] Those candid remarks manifested the contempt Arab leaders harbored toward Palestinians and their own subjects. It also underscored the prominence that pan-Islamic sympathies for Palestine would play in Saudi foreign policy decisions.

The Yom Kippur War of 1973

Egyptian President Anwar al-Sadat proposed several arrangements to peacefully reclaim the Sinai and its oil fields from Israel.[116] He and Faisal wanted Washington to pressure Israel into evacuating Arab territories seized during the Six Day War, as per UN Security Council Resolution 242, adopted in November 1967. After March 1969, however, an Egyptian-Israeli war of attrition along the Suez Canal derailed their efforts. Prospects worsened the following March when the Soviets supplied Sadat an advanced anti-aircraft missile defense system, accompanied by 1,500 military advisers and technicians. That figure later swelled beyond 10,000. The Soviet presence in Egypt dissuaded President Richard Nixon from pressuring Israel. Yet, even after Sadat expelled the Soviet personnel in July 1972, Washington remained reluctant to push its Israeli client. American foot-dragging infuriated King Faisal.

Self-preservation remained a primary consideration for the Saudi royal family, one in which Palestine and oil figured prominently. After 1969, the Saudis aided the PLO to forestall the danger of PLO attacks against the kingdom. Still, the Palestinian crisis raised Saudi concerns about terror operations on its assets and oil-production facilities. Palestinian refugees ignited the 1970 Black September war in Jordan; pro-Palestinian terrorists touched off the era's wave of airline hijackings; and Palestinian gunmen stormed the Saudi embassy in Khartoum in March 1973.[117]

Another background consideration involved the Organization of the Petroleum Exporting Countries (OPEC). Formed in September 1960, the cartel of oil-producing states collectively bargained to ration exports to oil-importing states. By the early 1970s, OPEC members wanted more influence over the ownership and activities of multinational oil companies operating in their territories. Saudi Arabia, with the world's largest crude reserves, was OPEC's swing producer and had the de facto final say in raising prices by cutting production. Hypothetically, if Arab oil ministers pursued collective action to decrease production and increase costs on targeted states, the Arab kingdom, as OPEC's leading member, felt compelled to wield the "oil weapon."

On the one hand, the world's largest energy producer had to appear supportive of pan-Arab causes against Israel, while on the other, the kingdom remained closely associated with the United States, the leading oil consumer and primary supporter of Israel. Those diverging interests were bound to collide. The pinnacle of hypocrisy occurred as another potential Arab-Israeli crisis loomed. President Sadat began to warn he could no longer accept peace talks' paralyzing stalemate and indicated his willingness to violently shatter the status quo. Meanwhile, in a *Foreign Affairs* article, State Department oil expert James E. Akins observed that in 1972 alone, Arab states threatened to use the oil weapon 15 separate times.[118] King Faisal joined the growing chorus in July 1973, telling American reporters he desired "a reasonable policy to bring a settlement," but "America's complete support for Zionism and against the Arabs makes it extremely difficult for us to continue to supply the United States with oil, or even to remain friends with the United States."[119] By August, Faisal began requesting detailed reports about the consequences of freezing oil production on consuming countries, in particular, the United States. That month, Sadat and Syria's Hafez al-Assad told Faisal that, if necessary, they would use force to reclaim Arab territories. Faisal reciprocated with an offer to defend

Muslim honor symbolically by coordinating an Arab response with the oil weapon.[120]

In Washington, however, skeptical officials refused to take those threats seriously. Secretary of Defense James Schlesinger dismissed Faisal's comments as "hot air."[121] Decisionmakers considered it lunacy that oil producers would sabotage their revenue stream or that Arabs would attack their militarily superior Israeli adversary. U.S. leaders also viewed the pro-West Saudi royal family, and the pro-West Shah of Iran, as the region's twin pillars of stable oil production and the moderate camp within OPEC. Besides, Arab and Saudi oil boycotts in 1956 and 1967 had failed to affect America's economic situation and that of its allies. Washington also relied heavily on Israeli intelligence, which downplayed the imminence of war and the competence of Arab soldiers. Those prevailing assumptions proved powerful.

On October 7, 1973—Yom Kippur, the Jewish calendar's holiest day—Egypt and Syria launched a surprise joint attack against Israel. An hour later, the Defense Intelligence Agency was *still* disputing reports of an Arab military buildup. The Soviets resupplied their Egyptian and Syrian clients, while Iraq, Libya, Algeria, Tunisia, Sudan, Morocco, Jordan, and Saudi Arabia joined the Arab effort with troops, tanks, and planes.[122] After two days, the Jewish state had suffered more casualties than during the Six Day War.

Various factors pulled U.S. officials in opposing directions in the course of aiding Israel. Save for Portugal and the Netherlands, America's European allies refused U.S. requests to use their bases or to over-fly their territories to send assistance. Because the Middle East accounted for 85 percent of oil consumed in Europe and 90 percent of oil consumed in Japan, they sought to avoid inflaming Arab indignity. Additionally, U.S. congressional probes over Watergate consumed the Nixon administration—the day President Nixon announced the airlift to Israel, October 10, Vice President Spiro Agnew tendered his resignation.

Another demand emanated from America's oil companies, which sponsored newspaper advertisements warning of too much support for Israel and emphasizing closer ties with Saudi Arabia. The chairmen of Exxon, Mobil, Texaco, and Socal urged President Nixon in a joint letter against aiding Israel, highlighting a "snowballing effect" in terms of Arab retaliation.[123] A back-channel U.S. envoy to Arab leaders, Jack McCloy, a partner to a firm whose clients included 22 chief executive officers of U.S. oil companies, had written years earlier in a letter to Secretary of State Dean Rusk: "The simple fact is our Israel policy is not operating in favor of our national interest in the Middle East."[124] His letter expressed the view of his petro-clients and reflected the conflicting impulses that animated America's Middle East policy.

Nixon and Kissinger tried mightily to respond to these competing pressures and interests. They concluded that an overwhelming Israeli victory would deepen Arab humiliation, increase Israel's bargaining leverage after the war, and make peace harder to reach. Such unvarnished realpolitik demonstrated another tendency in U.S.-Middle East statecraft: Washington weighed its interest to ensure Israel's survival against preventing, as Nixon later put it, "a hundred million Arabs hating us and providing a fishing ground not only for radicals but, of course, for the Soviets."[125]

As expected, U.S. aid to Israel provoked a swift Arab reaction. At more than 22,000 tons of equipment, the U.S. resupply to Israel (Operation Nickel Grass) exceeded the Berlin airlift. On October 16, after news of the resupply leaked, OPEC announced a 70 percent hike in oil prices. The following day, Arab oil ministers cut production by 5 percent and pledged to keep doing so each succeeding month.[126]

Despite the backlash, President Nixon agreed to give Israel an immediate military aid package of $2.2 billion on October 19. Saudi Arabia and other Arab states ceased exports to America and other supporters of Israel in retaliation.[127] The war finally ended following a UN-brokered ceasefire on October 22, although Nixon put U.S. military forces worldwide on high alert (Defcon III) on October 25 to deter the Soviets from stopping Israel's overwhelming counterattack against Egypt's Third Army. Eventually, through his step-by-step shuttle diplomacy, Secretary Kissinger mediated the Egyptian-Israeli Disengagement Agreement of January 1974 and the Syria-Israel Golan Heights Disengagement Agreement of May 1974. By March of that year, at Saudi Arabia's insistence, OPEC lifted its embargo.

Recycling Petrodollars

Known as the October War to the Arabs and the Yom Kippur War to the Israelis, the 1973 conflict challenged a number of prevailing

assumptions and prompted a major rethink of the U.S.-Saudi partnership. For many U.S. officials, the war diminished the credibility
of Israeli intelligence and the belief that its vaunted military superi-
ority would deter an Arab assault.

For the Saudis, though they failed to impose their will on America's Israel policy, they managed to convince many in Washington
to weigh Arab interests with sufficient seriousness, including U.S.
weapons manufacturers desiring new markets, Pentagon officials
seeking to reduce the per unit cost of arms and equipment, and diplomats urging stronger Arab-American relations. Eventually, the
Saudis began to take over Aramco, and by 1980, owned 100 percent
of the company. Finally, Riyadh became a secret conduit for Washington to restore diplomatic relations with Cairo, helping place the
most populous Arab state and the richest Arab state firmly in America's camp.[128]

For many Americans, the war and subsequent oil embargo reinforced the impression that oil-rich Arab despots held America hostage. In stark contrast to the picture that U.S. officials and pundits
painted, the energy crisis and lines of cars at gas stations stemmed
mainly from price controls and import quotas that limited the domestic energy market.[129] Nevertheless, Americans continued to over-
estimate the influence of Arab oil-production decisions, as the 1973
war and OPEC's embargo generated public interest in energy con-
servation, growing calls for energy independence, and substituting
away from Middle East oil. But for some U.S. officials and commentators, who during the war made veiled threats to seize Persian Gulf
oil militarily, the embargo inspired precisely the opposite reaction.[130]
They pushed to enhance U.S.-Saudi interdependence.

After the kingdom emerged from the oil embargo with more money
than it could spend, U.S. leaders sought to increase the Saudi stake in
the U.S. economy in order to prevent future dislocations of the global
economy. Toward that end, Secretary Kissinger and Treasury Secretary William E. Simon encouraged the royal family to lend, give, and
invest—"recycle"—revenue from oil sales—"petrodollars"—into
multinational companies. In the areas of science, infrastructure, education, agriculture, and others, foreign companies would help mod-
ernize the kingdom with Western goods and technology.[131] On June
8, 1974, the United States-Saudi Arabian Joint Commission on Economic Cooperation was born. A week later, after concluding discus-

sions with King Faisal in Washington, President Nixon articulated the benefits of heavy Saudi investment in the U.S. economy:

> If Saudi Arabia is strong and secure, as it will be, we will enhance the prospects for peace and stability throughout the Middle East and, in turn, throughout the world. . . . I would say that today American ties with Saudi Arabia have never been stronger and have never more solidly been based than they are now.[132]

Under joint cooperation, American civil servants advised their Saudi counterparts on governing the bureaucracies of a modern state, including planning development, improving financial data collection, and implementing proper banking standards. Those efforts proved less successful than inducing the Saudis to award contracts to American banks, construction and real estate firms, entrepreneurs, and other firms that channeled billions of petrodollars back into the U.S. economy. Joint security cooperation also recycled petrodollars with the sale of U.S.-manufactured military equipment. By the end of the decade, Saudi Arabia became one of the largest foreign investors in the U.S. economy, especially American banks, treasury bonds, and real estate.[133] Those lucrative business deals also increased Saudi Arabia's influence among American lobbyists, senior policymakers, business leaders, and retired diplomats.

Meanwhile, through its Islamic financial system, the kingdom poured petrodollars into the coffers of fellow Arab and Muslim states, Afro-Asian countries, and anti-communist rebel movements stretching from the Horn of Africa to the Philippines. Saudi-backed Islamic banks sprouted in Egypt, Sudan, Kuwait, Turkey, and elsewhere, helping to radicalize the region's politics by internationalizing the Muslim Brotherhood, Pakistan's Jama'at-e-Islami, and other Islamist movements, their writings, and audiotapes. Yusuf al-Qaradani, a cofounder of the Saudi-backed Faisal Islamic Bank of Egypt, condoned Palestinian attacks against Israel—even calling suicide bombings a legitimate act of self-defense. Wittingly or otherwise, Western financial institutions such as Citibank, Chase Manhattan, Goldman Sachs, Fannie Mae, Freddie Mac, and the U.S. Federal Reserve assisted Saudi Arabia's advancements in Islamic banking.[134]

Domestically, Saudi Arabia's immense wealth and rapid development failed to stem—even arguably helped to unleash—outbursts of religious extremism. A young Saudi prince shot and killed King Faisal on March 25, 1975. Some believe the assassin, Faisal's nephew, sought to avenge the death of his brother, whom Saudi government forces had killed a decade earlier as he tried to destroy Riyadh's television transmitter. The introduction of television had rattled rigid Wahhabi conservatives. Whatever the assassin's motive, the authorities beheaded him publicly. Crown Prince Khalid[135] became prime minister, and Crown Prince Fahd[136] oversaw domestic and foreign policy.[137] Notwithstanding that smooth succession, the royal family would face foreign and domestic disorder from even more extremists, and the final period of U.S.-Saudi Cold War relations is best understood in that context.

The Global Spread of Saudi Conservatism

In 1979, three major shocks convulsed the Saudi royal family and carried substantial political consequences for American national interests. The first occurred on January 16, 1979, when Iran's Anglo-American-installed Shah Mohammad Reza Pahlavi fled for Egypt after facing massive demonstrations, and even riots, against his tyrannical reign. For Washington, Iran's tumult justified the creation of combat-ready, rapidly deployable military units known as the Rapid Deployment Force, which by 1983, expanded into the theater-level U.S. Central Command, covering America's military responsibility in a vast region from Egypt to Kyrgyzstan. Despite Washington's "fly-in" of a dozen F-15 fighters to Saudi Arabia—which came three months after Riyadh's request—President Jimmy Carter announced the planes were unarmed. Washington's inability to reinstall the Shah, combined with sending unarmed jets, disturbed the royal family and prompted questions about the sincerity of Washington's security guarantee. Moreover, the threats befalling the kingdom would grow even more staggering.[138]

Arriving in Tehran on February 1, after years of exile in Paris, radical Shiite clerical leader Grand Ayatollah Ruhollah Khomeini rose to power and ignited a dangerous religious fervor across the region. His ascendance also kindled simmering resentments between Arabs and Persians, Sunnis and Shiites. As in this broadcast, Radio Tehran's shortwave Arabic channel beamed virulent anti-Saudi propaganda into Shiite towns in northeastern Saudi Arabia:

> The ruling regime in Saudi Arabia wears Muslim clothing, but inwardly represents the U.S. body, mind, and terrorism (*sic*). Funds are robbed from the people and squandered . . . for the luxurious, frivolous, and shameless way of life of the Saudi royal family and its entourage.[139]

Khomeini's propaganda directly challenged the royal family's spiritual authority, declaring Islam and hereditary kingship inherently incompatible. He emboldened disaffected Shiite minorities in Sunni-ruled Bahrain, Kuwait, and Saudi Arabia to rebel against their Sunni oppressors. On October 22, with turmoil gripping the region, President Carter allowed the Shah to enter America for cancer treatment. Two weeks later, revolutionary Islamist students stormed the American Embassy in Tehran and held 52 diplomats captive.

Radicals in Saudi Arabia tried to replicate the crisis in 1979's second major convulsion. During dawn prayers on November 20, a procession of approximately 500 mourners carrying coffins entered Mecca's Grand Mosque, a common sight as many pilgrims travel to the holy city to bless their dead. These mourners, though, set down the coffins, opened the lids, and took out a stockpile of grenades and assault rifles. They chained shut the doors of the stadium-sized, seven-acre mosque and locked the nearly 100,000 worshippers inside. Hostage ringleader and former Saudi National Guardsman Juhayman al-Utaybi had convinced several hundred Islamic University of Medina students—many of them Egyptian and Yemeni and more extreme than Saudi government-backed puritans—that his brother-in-law, Mohammed Abdullah al-Qahtani, was the messiah (*Mahdi*) returned to Earth to save Muslims from Western impurities. The Sunni zealots showed that Saudi Arabia was susceptible to revolutionary upheaval. They also represented the blend of Saudi Wahhabi extremism and Muslim Brotherhood jihadism. Matters got worse. The Saudi government evacuated the city and imposed a press blackout, which the State Department inadvertently undermined by releasing a press briefing. Over Mecca's loudspeakers, al-Utaybi called for bans on radio, television, and soccer and upbraided

Saudi rulers as "drunkards" who led "a dissolute life in luxurious palaces" and "squandered the state's money."[140]

His criticism struck a chord, as many ordinary Saudis and Wahhabi guardians of the religious establishment did view many royal family members and emirs as corrupt and decadent. After Saudi Army and National Guard units failed repeatedly to break the militants' defenses, with snipers in minarets picking off security forces, the kingdom turned to French counterterrorism commandos. After an instant conversion to Islam, as non-Muslims are strictly forbidden from Mecca, they fought the militants room-by-room in the mosque's underground vaults and chambers. Meanwhile, Saudi units callously exposed the hostages to indiscriminate lethal force, dropping grenades and canisters of disabling gas into rooms and rolling in M-113 armored personnel carriers into the shrine. The two-week bloodbath killed over 200 pilgrims, troops, and radicals and wounded 500 more. In a fitting spectacle of Saudi conservatism at its finest, the regime publicly decapitated al-Qahtani and his 63 surviving coconspirators in the largest mass execution in Saudi history.[141]

The gory standoff in Mecca marked an ominous turning point for the kingdom. The Wahhabi ulema, in its fatwa allowing the use of force inside the Grand Mosque, demanded that more of the kingdom's oil wealth go to spreading Wahhabism globally. The royal family obliged. Threatened by prospective domestic upheaval, it poured billions into the ulema and ambitious mosque-building campaigns. According to former U.S. Ambassador Richard Murphy, "The royal family decided then and there that no one would outflank them on the right."[142]

Already the Arab world's most traditional society, Saudi Arabia embraced an even more strident agenda at home. It fully unleashed its *mutawwa'in*, the ultra-conservative morality police. They flogged women in shopping malls for being improperly cloaked, charged them with prostitution for socializing with men who were not their relatives, and herded men into mosques to comply with the five daily prayers. They broke into private homes and businesses to destroy satellite dishes. And in their quest to stamp out sinfulness, heresy, and carnal sins, *mutawwa'in* even blacked out faces in advertisements and forbade the sale of children's dolls for their human representations.[143] Notwithstanding President Carter's professed commitment to humanitarian values elsewhere in the world, he (like his predecessors) generally acquiesced to the kingdom's subjugation of its citizens and illiberal worldview that inflicted social repression, political intimidation, and daily misery.

The royal family stepped up its efforts to outstrip religious opponents after 1979's third major convulsion: the Soviet Union's invasion of Afghanistan. Decades earlier, in a study commissioned by President Eisenhower, U.S. officials had deemed a Soviet takeover of the landlocked, Central Asian state as practically irrelevant to Washington.[144] That assessment apparently vanished in the mid 1970s. By then, the United States, Saudi Arabia, Pakistan, and Iran (pre-1979) tried to mobilize Afghan Islamists against the political and social modernization efforts of Afghan monarch Zahir Shah and left-leaning Prime Minister Mohammad Daoud.[145]

When Afghan Marxists seized power in Kabul in April 1978, Saudi leaders expressed concern to U.S. diplomats over a communist "pincer movement" encompassing Central Asia, the Horn of Africa, and the southern Arabian Peninsula.[146] National Security Advisor Zbigniew Brzezinski warned President Carter that the Soviets might use Afghanistan as a launching pad for territorial aggression elsewhere in the region.[147] Against nationalist enemies, the Saudi kingdom served more or less the same purpose for Washington. But by December, the Saudis faced their most definitive Soviet danger. The communist superpower sent 80,000 troops to prop up its faltering client regime in Kabul, which put Moscow in striking range of Iranian and Saudi oil fields. President Carter's January 1980 State of the Union Address presented Washington's most declarative public commitment to protect Persian Gulf oil for the industrial world:

> The Soviet effort to dominate Afghanistan has brought Soviet military forces to within 300 miles of the Indian Ocean and close to the Straits of Hormuz, a waterway through which most of the world's oil must flow. The Soviet Union is now attempting to consolidate a strategic position, therefore, that poses a grave threat to the free movement of Middle East oil.

He continued:

> Let our position be absolutely clear: An attempt by any

outside force to gain control of the Persian Gulf region will be regarded as an assault on the vital interests of the United States of America, and such an assault will be repelled by any means necessary, including military force.[148]

Carter's stern declaration relieved the Saudis, who moved to galvanize opposition to Afghanistan's communist occupiers that month at the Islamic conference in Islamabad. But Carter's speech did little to satisfy the American people. Many lost faith in the White House incumbent, who besides presiding over an ailing economy, appeared to horrendously mishandle foreign threats that persistently challenged American power. To rescue their country from its malaise, voters that November elected a staunch, anti-communist president.

Battles over Weapons

Carter's successor, Ronald Reagan, recommitted America's protection to Saudi Arabia at an October 1981 press conference. He stated the following when asked how he would prevent a repeat of the Iranian revolution in the Saudi kingdom:

> There is no way, as long as Saudi Arabia and the OPEC nations there in the East—and Saudi Arabia's the most important—provide the bulk of the energy that is needed to turn the wheels of industry in the Western World, there's no way that we could stand by and see that taken over by anyone that would shut off that oil.[149]

The president's response, though seemingly forthright, avoided the thrust of the question. Reagan sought to prevent the Saudi regime's demise. As did Crown Prince Fahd, who the following June ascended to the Saudi throne and wanted to limit the secularism accompanying the kingdom's modernization. He believed the Shah's modernizing "White Revolution" in the 1960s and early 1970s precipitated his downfall.[150] But by limiting secularism, combined with ongoing Saudi efforts to outshine religious radicals, the kingdom merely constituted a Sunni fundamentalist mirror image of the Shiite theocracy in Iran—a puritanism wildly volatile and ultimately uncontrollable.

Just weeks after Reagan's press conference, extremists led by a member of Egypt's Islamist group al-Jihad (Sacred Combat) assassinated pro-American President Anwar Sadat. His domestic economic reforms, brutal crackdowns on critics, and controversial peace negotiations with Israel alienated Egyptians, but he had also ushered in his country's religiously conservative shift. Sadat welcomed the Saudi-backed Faisal Islamic Bank of Egypt and the Muslim Brotherhood's Saudi-backed Al Taqwa Bank. He assumed the title of "Believer-President," began and ended his speeches with Quarnic verses, and fought the 1973 Arab-Israeli war under an Islamic banner of the "War of Ramadan." Cairo's al-Azhar University forged arrangements with Saudi Islamists, and many Egyptians working in Saudi Arabia returned home "Wahhabi-cized." The way of life in Egypt gradually changed, and long-time visitors noticed its Islamist shift.[151] It signaled the rising dominance of Saudi-Wahhabist ideology and how extremists focused on one target could quickly turn back on their patron.

Regional turmoil, including the September 1980 outbreak of war between Iran and Iraq, forced Saudi Arabia to rectify its military deficiencies. The results were the trade-and-security focused Gulf Cooperation Council with neighboring conservative and Sunni-ruled regimes, along with spending billions of dollars on U.S. construction services to expand Saudi air bases and port facilities.[152] Pro-Israel members of Congress, however, tried to block the sales of advanced American armaments to Riyadh that Saudi officials deemed critical for their security. Reagan thought selling some weapons would not materially affect the Arab-Israeli balance of power, whereas many on Capitol Hill argued that the weapons would either enhance Riyadh's capacity to wage war against Israel or migrate to other Islamist states.

"It is not the business of other nations to make American foreign policy," admonished President Reagan in response to Israeli efforts to pressure Congress.[153] These political battles regarding weapons to Saudi Arabia had erupted before: in 1976 over the transfer of Maverick air-to-ground missiles and in 1978 concerning the sale of F-15 fighter-bombers. By autumn 1981, controversy flared again about a proposed $8.5 billion arms sale that included five all-weather surveillance and command-and-control reconnaissance planes. Reagan expended considerable effort to ensure congressional authorization, meeting individually with 75 senators to close the deal. Although lawmakers narrowly approved the sale, the weapons battles continued and eroded the trust underpinning the U.S.-Saudi partnership.[154] Such sharp policy disagreements between the White House and Congress stemmed at least in part from the legal basis of the U.S.-Saudi alliance itself. The U.S. Constitution requires the advice and consent of the Senate regarding treaties; however, consecutive administrations evaded that requirement through tacit security arrangements with Riyadh that arose not from a formal defense treaty but rather through executive order.

Few leaders asked whether the cumulative result of U.S. assistance packages and repeated military deployments diminished rather than enhanced the kingdom's incentive to expand its defensive capabilities. Saudi Arabia depended upon non-Muslim foreigners to defend it from Colonel Nasser's Arab nationalists in the 1950s and 1960s, from Ayatollah Khomeini's Shiite radicals in the 1970s and 1980s, and from Saddam Hussein's Iraqi soldiers in the early 1990s. America's heavy military profile arguably compromised, to a high degree, the House of Saud's religious legitimacy (see chapter 13). Some Saudi princes saw weaknesses in the kingdom's reliance on the United States for its security. Indeed, the Saudi government ruled out soliciting the CIA's help during the siege in Mecca; Riyadh's lack of confidence in that agency was apparent when Saudi head of intelligence Prince Turki[155] said that strict congressional restrictions under President Carter had "emasculated" the CIA's operational capacity.[156] The kingdom saw congressional impediments to arms purchases as further eroding the credibility of the White House's pledge of protection.

As lawmakers reduced, stalled, and canceled proposed weapons sales, senior decisionmakers began circumventing Congress altogether. That evasion escalated from weapons sales to large-scale covert operations.[157] In the mid-1970s, when congressional and White House scandals blocked CIA activities, then secretary of state Henry Kissinger approved Saudi Arabia's participation in the Safari Club. The organization, comprised of leading officials from the external spy agencies of Britain, France, Saudi Arabia, Egypt, Turkey, Morocco, and Iran (pre-1979), led efforts to counter Soviet-backed Marxist movements in the Near East and North Africa. The Saudis pumped their oil riches into movements and causes in Angola, Chad, Sudan, Eritrea, Somalia, Jordan, North Yemen, Djibouti, Uganda, Mali, Nigeria, Guinea, Pakistan, Bangladesh, and other countries.[158]

Even Latin America emerged as a prominent front for high-level, U.S.-Saudi covert activities. Congress forbade the Pentagon and the CIA in December 1982 from providing military equipment, training, or advice "for the purpose of overthrowing" Nicaragua's leftist Sandinista regime.[159] The House Intelligence Committee voted the following May to cut all U.S. aid to the rebel Contras. Reagan's National Security Advisor Bud McFarlane, at the behest of CIA Director William Casey, contacted the kingdom for assistance. Saudi ambassador to the United States, Prince Bandar, agreed to put $1 million dollars a month into a Miami bank account for the Contras, a figure that eventually swelled to $32 million.[160] Such anti-leftist, U.S.-targeted, and Saudi-financed operations turned to mass violence in Afghanistan.

Headlong into Holy War

The USSR's invasion of Afghanistan in late 1979 shocked the Islamic world. After the revolution that roiled neighboring Iran and the insurrection that challenged its spiritual authority in Mecca, a Saudi royal family already dedicated to out-radicalizing religious radicals decided to reclaim its position as Islam's chief defender and back Afghanistan's rebels in their war of liberation. Saudi Arabia's General Intelligence Directorate (GID), alongside the CIA, flooded Afghanistan with billions in assistance—an estimated $4 billion alone from the Americans between 1982 and 1990, with the Saudis matching dollar for dollar. From 1979 to 1989, Saudi Arabia and the Gulf Arab sheikhdoms of Oman, Kuwait, Bahrain, Qatar, and the United Arab Emirates gave $600 million to Arab volunteer Osama bin Laden. The United States kept its funds in Pakistan's Bank of Credit and Commerce International (BCCI), a global network for money laundering, drug smuggling, and other skullduggery. Former Saudi intelligence chief Kamal Adham recalls then CIA director George H. W. Bush giving BCCI's activities "the official blessing."[161]

Through the Khyber Pass connecting Afghanistan and Pakistan, the CIA and GID, together with Pakistan's Directorate for Inter-

Services Intelligence (ISI), directed money and military hardware to the most radical and intolerant Afghan rebel factions (discussed in chapter 4). Most Afghan volunteers turned away from suicide bombings because of their extensive familial ties and patronage networks within the country. Non-Afghan volunteers had few such qualms. Foreign fighters from Saudi Arabia, Egypt, and elsewhere were willing martyrs, and hit soft targets like Kabul cinemas and cultural shows. According to Milton Bearden, a CIA field officer in Afghanistan from 1985 to 1989, many Muslim governments emptied their prisons and sent their criminals off to jihad hoping they would become martyrs. The Saudi kingdom disseminated flyers and pamphlets urging its youths to join the jihad; an estimated 12,000 complied. Saudi national airlines even gave a 75 percent discount to Afghan-bound volunteers.[162]

The kingdom soon became a haven for extremists. Blind Sheik Omar Abdul Rahman, a spiritual adviser to Egypt's Islamic Jihad and cofounder of the Saudi-backed Faisal Islamic Bank of Egypt, resided in the kingdom from 1977 through 1980 and was later convicted for his role in the February 1993 World Trade Center attack. Ayman al-Zawahiri, the future second-in-command and leader of al Qaeda, dwelled in the kingdom in the 1980s. Palestinian activist Abdullah Azzam, founder of al Qaeda's predecessor, Mekhtab al Khidemat (the Office of Services), was on the faculty of King Abdulaziz University. In the early and mid-1980s, Azzam toured across the United States—26 states total—recruiting for holy war. In Afghanistan, he received funding from Saudi intelligence, the Mecca-based Muslim World League, and Saudi princes. But he also called for jihad beyond Afghanistan—in Palestine, Burma, Somalia, Lebanon, Chad, the Philippines, and elsewhere.[163]

On the ground in Afghanistan and Pakistan, the Saudis also remained active. Sheikh Abdul bin Baz, the heliocentric-skeptic leader of the Wahhabi religious establishment, sent millions of dollars in cash and hundreds of volunteers to create an emirate in the isolated Kunar province abutting Pakistan's lawless tribal region. He managed the activities of Saudi charities, the International Islamic Relief Organization and the Muslim World League. In the Pakistani frontier city of Peshawar, which functioned as the Afghan rebellion's rear base, Saudi charities set up shop and built schools, hospitals, and battlefield medic services.[164] But even as private and public Saudi funds advanced Washington's anti-Soviet policies, the kingdom prioritized its own interests. When an Iraqi Mirage fighter attacked the American frigate USS *Stark* in 1987, the Saudis refused U.S. requests to intercept the Iraqi aircraft. The Saudis supported Iraq in its war with Iran, and 37 Americans lost their lives.[165]

U.S. deference to Saudi wishes appeared to pay off when Soviet troops withdrew from Afghanistan in defeat on February 15, 1989. But after the anti-Soviet holy war emerged a miasma of stateless renegades. International guerillas long-supplied with U.S. and Saudi money, weapons, and training sought new ventures in Chechnya, Sudan, Bosnia, and—ultimately—America. Other fighters returned to their home countries to topple their apostate regimes.

Well after the withdrawal of Soviet forces from Afghanistan, and the subsequent collapse of the Soviet Union itself, Saudi Arabia continued to export its Wahhabi religious doctrines and social traditions throughout the Islamic world. In mid-1995, a classified Federal Bureau of Investigation intelligence report listed the semiofficial Saudi government charity, the International Islamic Relief Organization, and the largest Saudi-government sponsored religious charity, the Muslim World League, as important sources of a new generation of Sunni Islamic extremists.[166] By the 2011 Arab Spring, when radical uprisings and calls for self-determination bloomed across the Middle East and North Africa, the long-time Saudi-backed Muslim Brotherhood movement emerged as the most highly organized political force in Egypt, Tunisia, Jordan, and Syria—a reflection of the Cold War past became a harbinger of the region's future.

In Afghanistan, the war continued to reverberate. The medieval-style Taliban regime, a Sunni-Pashtun dominated movement backed by Riyadh and Islamabad, assumed power in September 1996. Its harboring of al Qaeda, despite the group's responsibility for the 9/11 attacks, prompted the 2001 U.S.-led invasion. The Taliban regime echoed the Saudi kingdom's overzealous condemnation of the human spirit, destroying depictions of human images in photos and statues, outlawing singing and dancing, and amputating limbs for thievery. Taliban jurists also sentenced homosexuals and apostates to public executions. The ruthless regime even repurposed anti-Soviet, jihadist-era schoolbooks developed by the University of Nebraska at Omaha and federally funded by the U.S. Agency for International Development, scratching out human figures and keeping violent images and pictures of Kalashnikovs.[167] Tellingly, Saudi-financed religious schools also flourished. In the Pakistan-based Islamic seminary Dar-ul-Uloom Haqqania, from which eight Taliban ministers arose, a sign in one classroom read: "A Gift of the Kingdom of Saudi Arabia."[168]

Conclusion

From Roosevelt to Reagan, the United States protected the Kingdom of Saudi Arabia, while Riyadh provided Washington and its industrialized allies preferred access to its crude. That tacit oil-for-security partnership set in motion more expansive policies. U.S. foreign policy planners crafted bilateral relations around the importance of military bases, lucrative business ties, and mutual hostility toward leftists, communists, and otherwise uncooperative leaders. As top American leaders expressed their avowed commitment to democracy, human rights, and the rule of law, they deliberately ignored the realities of Saudi culture and its repressive, socially reactionary, anti-Semitic regime.

Although that arrangement neither alone nor primarily led to the rise of Islamist fanaticism, their Islamic-Christian alliance played a major role in the region's radicalization and destabilizing disintegration. The U.S.-Saudi Cold War alliance sacrificed America's commitment to liberalism for the sake of security and undermined both. The virulent strain of Wahhabi Islam, not shared by a majority of Muslims, particularly beyond the Arabian Peninsula, became an assertive ideological force across the Muslim world. It transcended ethnic and linguistic cleavages to become a malignant force defining the beginning of the 21st century.

2. From "Golden Chain" to Arab Spring: The Sordid Tale of U.S.-Saudi Relations

One of the strongest beliefs about American foreign policy in the Middle East has been that policymakers base most political engagements and military interventions upon the geostrategic value of oil. Former Federal Reserve Chairman Alan Greenspan caught flack when he said of the 2003 U.S.-led invasion of Iraq, "I am saddened that it is politically inconvenient to acknowledge what everyone knows: the Iraq war is largely about oil."[1] James A. Baker, secretary of state in George H. W. Bush's administration, went further. He argued in the context of longtime U.S. ally, the Kingdom of Saudi Arabia: "I worked for four administrations under three presidents. And in every one of those, our policy was that we would go to war to protect the energy reserves in the Persian Gulf."[2] That "oil-for-security" thesis not only diverged from well-known facts about contemporary energy markets but also overlooked the unforeseen consequences from an alliance in need of reexamination.

"It's been a huge recruiting device for al Qaeda," former deputy secretary of defense Paul Wolfowitz said of the 12-year U.S. troop presence at Prince Sultan Air Base in Riyadh, Saudi Arabia. That base served as Washington's command-and-control center for aerial patrols of Iraqi airspace, the so-called "no-fly zone," following the Persian Gulf War (1990–1991). "In fact if you look at [Osama] bin Laden, one of his principal grievances was the presence of so-called crusader forces on the holy land, Mecca and Medina."[3]

As Wolfowitz explains above, Osama bin Laden, who had emerged from the dark recesses of Afghanistan's decade-long rebellion against its Soviet occupation (1979–1989), turned his focus westward, invoking the presence of U.S. troops on holy soil to rally war-hardened militants to attack U.S. allies and interests across the globe. But often unmentioned in discussions of U.S.-Saudi relations was his movement's web of support from private Saudi donors, financial facilitators, and Saudi-based charitable foundations. That funding system, collectively called the "Golden Chain," overlapped with the Saudi monarchy's multidecade campaign to spread its ultra-conservative brand of Sunni Islam, called Wahhabism in the West and Salafism by its followers. Once confined to the Arabian Peninsula, Salafism gained significant influence in all countries with large Muslim populations, where its unique interpretation of Islam promoted some of the most oppressive social restrictions and meta-morphosed alongside other rigid Islamist doctrines to become the ideological source of Salafi extremism exemplified by al Qaeda ("the base") and the Islamic State of Iraq and Syria (ISIS).

Reams of documentation from U.S. government investigations, pre-viously classified documents from George Washington University's National Security Archive, and first-hand accounts from former U.S. national security and intelligence officials show that the United States government suffered massive policy and intelligence failures in the years, months, and even days leading up to 9/11: egregious aviation security lapses, communication breakdowns between the Federal Bu-reau of Investigation (FBI) and the Central Intelligence Agency (CIA), and a reluctance among cabinet-level U.S. officials, collectively known as "the Principals," to pressure their counterparts in the kingdom about Saudi charitable assistance and terrorist financing. Revelations about 9/11's perpetrators jolted the U.S.-Saudi alliance: 15 of the 19 hijackers were Saudi nationals; their murderous conspiracy was as-sisted by an exile of one of the kingdom's most powerful and wealthi-est families; and private Saudi support helped sustain much of the terrorist activity that led up to and followed the 9/11 attacks.

Following the 2003 Iraq War, the 2011 Arab Spring, and the 2013 consolidation of ISIS, when the Arab Sunni kingdom feared encir-clement from Persian Shiite Iran and its allies, Saudi-inspired and funded Salafists blossomed across North Africa and the Middle East. They acquired Saudi weapons and support in Iraq, Lebanon, and Syria; formed factions and political parties in Bahrain, Kuwait, Al-geria, Libya, and Yemen; and won pluralities in post-revolutionary elections held in Tunisia, Morocco, and Egypt. Washington's long-standing, oil-rich ally made Salafism and its reactionary worldviews far broader than either bin Laden or the violent religious nationalism he spawned.

Issues surrounding the U.S.-Saudi alliance and the unintended byproducts of that association warrant considerable attention, especially given the consequences to the United States. Those consequences include the blood and treasure expended to fight terrorism, the fractious domestic political debates that Washington's anti-terrorism policies have generated, the scope of U.S. government surveillance in the struggle against terrorism, and the troubling short-term distraction of the Middle East from longer-term great-power politics. The American people—a major target of international terrorism—deserve to know the truth about the U.S.-Saudi alliance. Indeed, misguided policies and costly intractable wars partly reflect a public too ill-equipped to refute the misinformation given to them by officials vested in continuing the Middle East status quo. Until the public fully understands the U.S.-Saudi partnership, it will fail to comprehend the unexpected dangers that come from that alliance, which has enjoyed decades of Washington's political validation and military protection.

The Golden Chain

As a 2006 U.S. State Department report to Congress concluded, "Saudi donors and unregulated charities have been a major source of financing to extremist and terrorist groups over the past 25 years."[4] How those donors and charities grew to become the leading source of terrorist financing relates directly to the oil-rich kingdom's centrality in the Islamic world.

As the "Custodian of the Two Holy Mosques" in Mecca and Medina, the holiest sites in Islam, the kingdom holds tremendous sway over the global community of Muslims (*umma*). For decades, its religious scholars and conservative citizens devoted themselves to exporting their country's puritanical Salafist movement within Sunni Islam. During the Cold War, Riyadh founded and partially funded transnational charities that spread its austere religiosity and promoted pan-Islamism against pan-Arab nationalists in Egypt, Iraq, and Syria, and later, revolutionary Islamists in Libya, Iran, and at home. As noted in chapter 5, Saudi-based charities, including the Muslim World League (1962), the World Assembly of Muslim Youth (1972), the International Islamic Relief Organization (1979), and many others, underwrote the building of mosques, religious schools, medical facilities, potable water systems, and other social projects and programs to educate poor orphans and feed hungry refugees.

From Angola to Nicaragua, and most notably, Afghanistan—a longtime target of Saudi-Salafist proselytizing and the country from which the 9/11 attacks were planned—Riyadh's charitable activities often overlapped U.S.-Saudi policies that backed anti-communist insurgencies. From 1979 to 1989, under Operation Cyclone, the CIA—alongside the external spy agencies of Saudi Arabia's General Intelligence Directorate (GID) and Pakistan's Inter-Services Intelligence Directorate (ISI)—armed, trained, and financed Afghanistan's most radical guerilla commanders to ensnare the large ground combat forces of the Soviet Union. The conflict's most infamous religious volunteers from the Arab world, the "Arab Afghans," included Palestinian militant and Muslim Brotherhood scholar Abdullah Azzam—who established the seemingly innocuous Mekhtab al Khidemat (the "Services Office") in 1984, the precursor to al Qaeda—and Saudi national and religious philanthropist Osama bin Laden—who between 1980 and 1983 distributed cash donations to anti-Soviet rebels.[5] Azzam reportedly exposed bin Laden to the concept of transnational jihad, which insisted that all Muslims had a religious obligation to expel unbelievers from Muslim lands.[6] Accordingly, bin Laden, who later formed a committee within the Services Office promoting media and education, used graphic depictions and video imagery in charity marketing to promote the Afghan rebels and deify innocent orphans.[7]

Director of the GID General Prince Turki al'Faisal and longtime Saudi ambassador to America Prince Bandar bin Sultan claimed their government had little direct contact with bin Laden during this period. However, compelling evidence suggests more routine interaction.[8] Ahmed Badeeb, bin Laden's former high school teacher and Turki's former chief of staff, claimed bin Laden "had a strong relation with the Saudi intelligence and with our embassy in Pakistan."[9] During the war's early years, according to bin Laden's former friend, Jamal Khashoggi, GID supported "the military part," while private religious philanthropists would "support the humanitarian and relief work."[10]

Among a hoard of al Qaeda documents discovered in Bosnia after 9/11, a 1988 memorandum identified wealthy and influential Saudi families, financial backers, and one former Saudi government minister as early supporters of bin Laden—the "Golden Chain," as his movement called it.[11] Private donations for the purchase of medicine and food blended with funds to buy Kalashnikovs and rocket-propelled grenades. The Saudi government collected charitable giving required of all observant Muslims (*zakat*)—one of Islam's five pillars—and used a portion of the donations for charities to build religious schools and mosques around the world. Some charities wittingly helped bin Laden. Sympathetic facilitators infiltrated other organizations covertly, using mosque and civic-center charity boxes to mask the transfer of funds.[12] Human couriers also moved cash within and across borders and relied on a system of paperless funds (*hawala*) similar to Western Union.[13] As Azzam said before his death in 1989, the year the Soviets withdrew in defeat from Afghanistan, "Saudi [Arabia] is the only country which stood by the Afghani jihad as a government and peope."[14] However, another war in the Muslim world soon turned the Arab Afghans and their Saudi benefactors into mortal enemies.

On August 2, 1990, Iraq invaded Kuwait. Saudi Arabia, on Iraq's southern border, lay militarily vulnerable despite having spent billions on sophisticated American weaponry and equipment.[15] Bin Laden offered to save the cradle of Islam, laying out his plan in a 60-page paper offering to recruit and lead his guerilla-trained jihadist veterans against Saddam Hussein.[16] Instead, based upon a religious edict (fatwa) from the Council of Senior Ulema, a select group of some 20 scholars of Islamic law appointed by the monarch, within a matter of days Saudi Arabia's King Fahd bin Abdulaziz Al Saud welcomed the offer of protection from U.S. President George H. W. Bush, who then dispatched 2,300 U.S. paratroopers to the Arabian Peninsula under Operation Desert Shield.[17]

The following month, Secretary of Defense Dick Cheney claimed before the Senate Armed Services Committee that Iraq would control about 20 percent of the world's known oil reserves by conquering Kuwait. That position would give Saddam Hussein "a position to be able to dictate the future of worldwide energy policy" and a "stranglehold on our economy and on that of most other nations of the world."[18]

Secretary Cheney furnished no evidence to support his claim about Iraq's prospective domination of "worldwide energy policy." Uncertainty over the erratic dictator's intentions did loom large, but the commitment to combat was divorced from the fundamental realities of international commodity markets. Indeed, the United States acquires energy resources from many places, including its own hemisphere, because market forces, rather than a specific supplier, determine the supply of oil.[19] Other oil producers could have replaced the lost oil capacity even if a major long-term disruption occurred—a nightmare scenario that was unlikely.[20] Another fear, as President Bush wrote in his diary on August 2 about his reason for scrambling U.S. fighter squadrons to the Gulf, was "that the Kuwaiti puppet government set up by Iraq would try to move billions of dollars out of Western banks and out of U.S. banks illegally."[21]

Saddam, a demonic figure renowned for his ruthlessness, presumably had few incentives to stifle the availability of oil, particularly if self-enrichment motivated his pillaging. His country's bloody eight-year war against Iran—despite varying degrees of support to him from Washington and Riyadh—ended in 1988 with a stalemate and left Iraq depleted.[22] Some critics later claimed that the Bush administration misrepresented the threat by vastly overestimating the number of Iraqi troops poised on Saudi Arabia's borders: not 547,000 troops, as originally claimed, but barely one-third of that, about 183,000.[23] President Bush had also equated Saddam to Adolf Hitler, casting him as the archvillain in a millenarian dichotomy between "good and evil."[24] In any event, international sanctions and diplomatic efforts failed to remove Iraqi forces from Kuwait, and in January 1991 the U.S. Senate authorized a more robust military deployment under Operation Desert Storm. That month, when President Bush announced in a televised address that the United States and a coalition of 34 countries, including Arab states, had begun air attacks against Iraqi forces, Bush castigated the dictator: "Saddam Hussein systematically raped, pillaged, and plundered a tiny nation."[25]

A week after the U.S.-led coalition completed its rout of Iraqi forces on February 28, President Bush asserted that America's motives were altruism and the mediation of international conflict.[26] Before a joint session of Congress, he declared that America's intervention in the conflict would usher "the very real prospect of a new world order . . . A world where the United Nations, freed from cold war stalemate, is poised to fulfill the historic vision of its founders."[27]

America's Founders had elaborated a different, and far more humble and pragmatic, philosophy—one that cautioned against foreign entanglements. Conversely, Bush asserted that the continued triumph of global economic and political freedom in the post-Soviet age depended on U.S. global leadership to enforce nonaggression and international law. Most important, in a line of thought that led many U.S. leaders to conflate America's strategic and moral interests, Bush clearly implied that stamping out a recalcitrant thug such as Saddam through United Nations (UN) multilateralism demonstrated the value of alliances and the benefits of U.S. dominance and credibility. To some in Saudi Arabia, however, Washington harbored malicious motives.

The arrival of more than 500,000 U.S. soldiers, sailors, and airmen on Saudi soil provoked tremendous discontent in the most closed of Arab societies. The liberation of Kuwait indicated how U.S.-led intervention in the Middle East could promote democracy, and the kingdom's liberal-leaning business elites, journalists, women, and university professors called for political reforms.[28] But in some circles, the U.S. troop presence on Muslim holy land also triggered religious fervor, political resistance, social panic, and rabid patriotism. To bin Laden and other Saudi Islamists, the calls for liberal reform confirmed their suspicions that the U.S.-Saudi alliance—and King Fahd's invitation to foreign, predominately Christian, troops to save the holiest sites in Islam—would lead to mass secularization and corrupt their society's Islamic principles.[29] Humiliated and outraged over Fahd's refusal to accept his rebellious legions, bin Laden left Saudi Arabia for Sudan in May 1991.

Many observers have come to identify the Persian Gulf War (1990–1991) as bin Laden's impetus to attack American interests. But it was the Afghan-Soviet War's preexisting financial and logistical network of private donors and charities that enabled bin Laden to launch his strikes against the Saudi regime, autocratic Arab rulers, and the West. "Financial jihad," as bin Laden later wrote, "likewise, is an obligation."[30]

In the years to come, bin Laden's name appeared on cassette tapes and jihadi promotional material in disparate locations: Eritrea, Kashmir, the Balkans, and the Philippines. Bin Laden paired his philanthropy with guerilla violence around the world by funding local Islamic insurgencies. Even before he left Afghanistan for Saudi Arabia in the late 1980s, he had trained and housed rebels fighting South Yemen's communist government.[31]

By May 1991, according to a report later recovered from its Illinois office, the Saudi relief organization Benevolence International

Foundation (BIF) had started services in Sudan. Around that same that time, bin Laden's movement also began training the Sudanese militia, Popular Defense Force, in guerilla war tactics against Sudanese Christians and animists.[32] The BIF's two closely linked, but separately incorporated, entities aided the Bosnian army and its irregular warfare unit, the Black Swans.[33] The U.S. Treasury Department would later designate BIF a racketeering enterprise supporting al Qaeda.[34] The movement's wealthy Saudi founder also extended moral support to independent acts of anti-American terror.

In February 1993 terrorists linked to bin Laden attacked the North Tower of the World Trade Center in New York City, killing six people and injuring more than a thousand. The following year, when the Saudi government revoked bin Laden's Saudi citizenship, bin Laden was financing rebels from a half-dozen countries at terrorist training camps in northern Sudan.[35] He praised Saudi pro-Hezbollah operatives who, in November 1995, detonated a car bomb that killed five Americans at the Saudi National Guard training center in Riyadh—the location from which more than one hundred U.S. Air Force fighter aircraft patrolled Iraq's southern no-fly zone under Operation Southern Watch. He also commended the June 1996 Khobar Towers bombing that killed 19 U.S. Air Force servicemen and injured more than three hundred others.[36]

Despite the terrorist financier's string of attacks and global reach, U.S. leaders only began paying serious attention to al Qaeda after January 1996. President Bill Clinton's National Security Advisor Tony Lake and National Coordinator for Security and Counterterrorism Richard Clarke pushed to create a special unit within the CIA's Counterterrorism Center to track bin Laden and his terrorist financing. Yet few policymakers or intelligence analysts truly understood radical Islam and the international scope of bin Laden's activities. Far fewer could exercise the necessary influence to pressure Riyadh to help bring bin Laden to justice.

Pre-9/11 Intelligence

Throughout the 1990s, the Principals, those cabinet-level U.S. officials charged with formulating high-level policies with the kingdom, were disinclined to ask too much from their Saudi counterparts about retarding extremism or terrorist financing. Meanwhile, bureaucratic turf wars within and among the Federal Bureau of Investigation, the Central Intelligence Agency, and other departments led the U.S. government's national security complex to miss preparations for the deadliest terror attacks on American soil.

Sudan, under heavy U.S. diplomatic pressure, expelled bin Laden in May 1996. The terrorist financier revitalized his Golden Chain funding stream after he, his militia, and their families fled to Afghanistan. That July, the U.S. Embassy in neighboring Pakistan reported the "existence of religious madrassas and other institutions, including youth training camps which could be spawning terrorism." It continued, "The most recent indications are that institutions of this nature are funded from Saudi Arabia."[37] U.S. intelligence had also uncovered links between the Saudi-based charity Al Haramain Islamic Foundation (HIF) and support for militant Islamist activity in Chechnya, Azerbaijan, the Balkans, and al Qaeda more generally.[38] As one of the most prominent al Qaeda–linked Saudi charities, which former U.S. officials described as the "United Way" of the kingdom, at one point it raised $40 to $50 million a year in contributions.[39]

As Saudi charities underwrote the building of thousands of mosques, missions, and branch offices in 50 countries across Africa, Asia, Europe, and North America, U.S. troops in the region remained forward deployed in Saudi Arabia, Kuwait, Bahrain, Diego Garcia, and Turkey, among other locations. In response, bin Laden's philosophy evolved. He began framing the stationing of U.S. troops in Saudi Arabia within the broader picture of U.S. military intervention and political interference across the Islamic world.[40] In his August 1996 fatwa, "Declaration of War against the Americans Occupying the Land of the Two Holy Places," he demanded the United States "desist from aggressive intervention against Muslims in the whole world" and exhorted the violent overthrow of Arab police states and corrupt Muslim tyrannies such as those in Morocco, Jordan, Egypt, Saudi Arabia, and other countries that were complicit in America's crimes.[41] Bin Laden deemed them un-Islamic, and hence, apostate.[42]

"A man with human feelings in his heart does not distinguish between a child killed in Palestine or Lebanon, in Iraq or in Bosnia," bin Laden told CNN in 1997. "So how can we believe your claims that you came to save our children in Somalia while you kill our children in all of those places?"[43] Bin Laden had taken to citing the more than "600,000 Iraqi children" killed, he claimed, by the U.S.-

led no-fly zone mission to control Iraqi airspace and the economic sanctions pushed by Washington.[44] While those measures certainly took a toll on innocent children, competing evidence also points to Saddam's diversion of $2 billion in humanitarian aid for the killing of Iraqi civilians. Regardless, bin Laden invoked the grievances perpetrated against innocent Muslims to exploit concepts of human rights and other basic values to delegitimize American policies. To bin Laden and his followers, the trail of civilian deaths that Washington's policies left in their wake vindicated the killing of American civilians. Even though the Quran explicitly forbids the taking of innocent lives and the murder of women and children, the American people, bin Laden claimed, "are not exonerated from responsibility" because they choose their government "despite their knowledge of its crimes."[45]

The punishments bin Laden wanted for America's crimes steadily expanded. By late February 1998, Ayman al-Zawahiri, the former head of Egyptian Islamic Jihad, the militant group that assassinated Anwar Al-Sadat, joined his militant forces with bin Laden' s under the banner International Islamic Front for Jihad on the Jews and Crusaders.[46] The movement, as it subsequently became known—al Qaeda—exhorted all Muslims to attack U.S. military and civilian targets anywhere in the world. It also talked ominously about "bringing the war home to America."[47] That May, bin Laden boasted, "I am confident that Muslims will be able to end the legend of the so-called superpower that is America."[48] Having observed America's ignominious departure from Lebanon in 1983 after Hezbollah bombed the U.S. Embassy and Marine barracks and its departure again from Somalia in 1993 after militants thought to be trained by bin Laden killed 18 U.S. servicemen, bin Laden saw America, as he said in May 1998 to ABC News, as being casualty averse—"just a paper tiger."[49]

Bin Laden effectively stood U.S. grand strategy on its head, turning U.S. foreign policy into a threat to U.S. national security. As opposed to a conventional war fought for limited aims, bin Laden's Salafi-inspired religious nationalism remained ostensibly a defensive war fought for unlimited aims. That was a critical point, and one not appreciated nearly enough. His zealotry and reactionary worldview, cited plentifully in the militant Islamist literature, seemed unstable: it went from evicting U.S. troops from Saudi Arabia to expelling U.S. troops from the entire region and stopping U.S. interference against all Muslims to calling for America's collapse. Even if Washington complied with al Qaeda's demands, bin Laden likely would have found other justifications for violence.

Regional experts, retired diplomats, military and intelligence officials, and investigative reporters analyzed those and other perceived injustices before, and especially after, 9/11. Like Cold War–era Kremlinology, their findings examine enemy doctrine, including the enemy's grotesque justifications for violence. Beneath such aims and depredations lie motives for understanding what specific interests and assets an enemy seeks to target. They can reveal secretive processes and indirect clues and point to approaches required among diplomatic, economic, military, and intelligence tools. In this case, such research contributed to a richer understanding of the iconic figure who possessed an exceptional ability to recruit from all over the world and attract millions of sympathizers to his violent extremism.

That inspiration and the ideology's ever-expanding transformation occurred as American leaders diverged over how much priority the cooperation with Saudi Arabia on counterterrorism should have over other mutual interests.

The Principals

As early as 1996, FBI Counterterrorism Chief John O'Neill believed bin Laden and al Qaeda threatened America's security. He also believed that powerful figures in the Saudi kingdom had close ties to bin Laden. Yet, according to O'Neill, America's dependence on Saudi oil seemingly gave the kingdom more leverage on Washington than Washington had on Riyadh.[50] American lawmakers had expressed similar concerns over Riyadh's financial power as early as 1979 and again in 1985 when U.S. Treasury officials refused to publicly divulge how much the Saudis held in U.S. securities. Critics feared those investments would give Saudi Arabia undue influence over U.S. foreign policy and erode America's political and economic independence.[51] That erosion may have occurred, but in less conspicuous ways.

In Washington, the most senior-level cabinet officials—a committee of the secretaries of state and defense, the director of the CIA, the chairman of the joint chiefs (and, under President Bush, often the vice president)—formulated U.S. policy toward Saudi Arabia. Collectively called "the Principals," many of those leaders formed close personal friendships with high-ranking Saudi leaders and members of the royal family. For example, former president George W. Bush recounted in his memoirs a 2002 meeting with Crown Prince Abdullah bin Abdulaziz Al Saud in Crawford, Texas. "The next day," wrote Bush, "I got a call from Mom and Dad. The crown prince had stopped in Houston to visit them."[52] Such casual interactions carried over into intelligence and diplomacy. In the late 1990s, CIA Director George Tenet reportedly traveled once a month from the CIA headquarters in Virginia to the nearby McLean home of Prince Bandar, the longtime Saudi ambassador to America.[53]

On the one hand, such personal relations can protect and advance America's official diplomatic partnerships by helping officials curry favor with powerful, well-connected foreign leaders in times of crisis or on matters of extraordinary importance. On the other hand, such cliquish insularity has the potential to discourage officials and policymakers from acknowledging certain realities. According to investigations by the 2004 National Commission on Terrorist Attacks upon the United States (the 9/11 Commission), lower-level U.S. officials with knowledge of private Saudi terrorist financing had no interaction with the Saudis. Higher-level U.S. officials who did, however, acceded to the strong Saudi preference to bypass the U.S. bureaucracy and "did not push the issue of terrorist financing because their concerns were different."[54] By 1997, the CIA analytical unit charged with monitoring bin Laden and al Qaeda issued a memorandum to CIA Director Tenet identifying Saudi intelligence as a "hostile service": the CIA term used to describe such entities as Cuban and Iranian intelligence.[55]

Perhaps out of a seeming reluctance to impute guilt, officials with greater influence failed to press their Saudi counterparts for more cooperation on terrorist financing. That reluctance could not have occurred at a more critical time. In early 1998, CIA surveillance and National Security Agency (NSA) eavesdropping revealed that bin Laden spent much of his time at Tarnak Farms, a compound in Kandahar, southern Afghanistan. Some in the agency developed a plan to capture bin Laden, while others proposed an immediate cruise missile strike. Tenet and Clarke, among others, objected and deemed the plans too risky. After canceling the operation, and underscoring the leverage of personal ties, Director Tenet flew to Saudi Arabia that May to seek Riyadh's help to capture bin Laden.[56]

Unfortunately, on that occasion, personal familiarity apparently failed to bear fruit. That June, Prince Turki met in Kandahar with Taliban spiritual leader Mullah Muhammad Omar. Allegedly, they agreed to explore ways to formally hand over bin Laden, and as down payment for the arrangement, the kingdom sent the Taliban 400 pick-up trucks and material assistance.[57] But on August 7, 1998, three months after Director Tenet's trip to Saudi Arabia, al Qaeda–rigged truck bombs blew up the U.S. Embassies in Kenya and Tanzania within five minutes of each other. The attack, eight years to the day after U.S. troop deployments to Saudi Arabia, killed 224 people and wounded more than 4,600 others.[58]

By the late 1990s and early 2000s, U.S. officials seemed to react to the repeated al Qaeda threats and attacks in a similar fashion: unsurprised, given existing intelligence, yet seemingly hapless and confused over how and when to respond. After the U.S. embassy attacks, President Clinton slapped sanctions on bin Laden and his organization and approved an order to launch cruise missile strikes against targets in Afghanistan and Sudan. The strikes hit largely abandoned camps, making it look, as Clinton's successor later wrote, "impotent and ineffectual."[59] To his credit, Clinton later claimed he inquired about a commando raid on al Qaeda training operations in Afghanistan, but senior U.S. military leaders recommended against it "perhaps because of Somalia."[60] That policy paralysis happened again in October 2000 after al Qaeda's attack on the USS *Cole*, which killed 17 American sailors in Yemen. Between a Special Forces operation shelved by the Pentagon and a bombing campaign of Afghanistan called off at the last minute due to unreliable intelligence, the White House, in the end, did nothing.[61]

According to Ahmad Zaidan, the Pakistan bureau chief for Al Jazeera television who interviewed bin Laden twice before 9/11, bin Laden wanted the USS *Cole* bombing to drag the Americans into Afghanistan and have fellow Muslims fight them as they did in Somalia and against the Soviets.[62] It is believed that Zawahiri, bin Laden's deputy, encouraged bin Laden to divert al Qaeda's emphasis from the "near enemy"—apostate Muslim states and societies—to the "distant enemy"—the United States and its Western allies.[63] In a policy developed before 9/11 and expounded upon thereafter, al

Qaeda now viewed its terrorism as a calculated maneuver to elicit U.S. and Western reprisals in Arab and Muslim lands, ensnaring them in protracted ground campaigns to the point of financial insolvency. Bin Laden envisioned a protracted ground campaign in the Afghan mountains. Rather than repelling U.S. troops, bin Laden's strategy welcomed them.

Another astonishing aspect of pre-9/11 Washington was the intra-agency turf wars that hamstrung America's intelligence bureaucracy over suspected Saudi terrorist assistance and financing. By nearly all accounts, problems at the FBI were particularly disturbing. Counterterrorism czar Richard Clarke described the efforts of more than 50 FBI field offices before 9/11 as "extremely poor and not coordinated," and former National Security Council official Paul Kurtz described his dealings with the pre-9/11 FBI as "totally infuriating."[64]

In the mid-1990s, the FBI reportedly declined 14,000 pages of documents from defecting Saudi diplomat Mohammed al-Khilewi that allegedly showed the Saudi regime's official support for terrorism.[65] In 2000, two years after FBI field offices had learned that a large number of Arabs were attending American flight schools, an al Qaeda recruit in New York who got cold feet told the FBI he was recruited to hijack passenger planes. Although he passed two lie detector tests, the FBI returned him to England.[66] Most infamously, Mawaf al-Hazmi and Khalid al-Mihdhar, two future 9/11 hijackers, had close and repeated contact with an FBI counterterrorist informant but nothing came of it.[67]

Another problem, as with the Principals, was conflicting objectives. After 9/11, a U.S. Department of Justice (DOJ) investigation of the FBI discovered that, by early 2000, FBI headquarters made counterterrorism the bureau's top concern: however, the FBI field office in San Diego, California, where Saudi Arabian national Omar al-Bayoumi had spent a "significant amount of time" with the two hijackers mentioned above, continued to pursue drug trafficking as its top concern.[68]

One FBI source opined that Bayoumi, an active member of San Diego's Muslim community, "must be an agent of a foreign power or an agent of Saudi Arabia." Regardless of the accuracy of that suspicion, an FBI case agent told the DOJ's Inspector General that "Saudi Arabia was not listed as a threat country and the Saudis were considered allies of the United States."[69] Most significant, a squad supervisor also told the DOJ's Inspector General that "before September 11, the Saudi Arabian government was considered an ally of the United States and that a report of an individual being an agent of the Saudi government would not have been considered a priority."[70] By this time, the CIA's bin Laden unit had already deemed Saudi intelligence "hostile."[71]

That discrepancy between the FBI and the CIA represented yet another problem with the passing of critical information. In the months leading up to the October 2000 USS *Cole* bombing, the perpetrators met in Kuala Lumpur, Malaysia. Among them were the two 9/11 hijackers. Although the FBI, according to the DOJ investigation, had several opportunities to uncover information on the plotters, the CIA, which had worked with the Malaysian authorities, did not share that information with the FBI.[72] Among its many findings, the DOJ investigation found "systemic problems" within the FBI and between the FBI and the CIA with the "gathering or passing of information" about the two 9/11 hijackers mentioned above.[73] From Kuala Lumpur the two aspiring hijackers flew first to Los Angeles then to San Diego. As 9/11 Commission member Senator Bob Kerrey (D-NE) revealed later during the commission's hearings, one of the biggest mistakes made after 1998 was "allowing al Qaeda to come inside the United States. . . . We continued to allow them to come to the United States."[74] Indeed, before 9/11, al Qaeda operatives traveled to Florida, Georgia, California, Arizona, and Virginia. Ostensibly, the U.S. State Department could have put the bombers' names on a terrorist watch list to stop them from entering the United States, but it was kept in the dark until August 24, 2001—less than three weeks before the 9/11 attacks and after the hijackers had already entered America.[75]

The ineffective handling of pre-9/11 intelligence called into question the strength of America's byzantine intelligence system. Michael Scheuer, with the CIA from 1982 to 2004 and the head of the CIA's bin Laden unit from 1996 to 1999, argued that leaders executing policy had underestimated al Qaeda and missed multiple opportunities to strike at bin Laden. Some setbacks involved political choices unrelated to the intelligence analytical process. For instance, in 1996, Sudan reportedly offered to arrest bin Laden and hand him to the Saudis, but the Saudis balked. U.S. diplomats privy to the details of the arrangement believed that other priorities dominated the U.S.-

Saudi alliance, including Washington's reliance on Saudi territory to patrol Iraq, and thus, "the White House did not press the Saudis very hard."[76]

Moreover, some Principals lacked focus on al Qaeda, a point confirmed in counterterrorism czar Richard Clarke's January 2001 memorandum that pleaded to incoming National Security Advisor Condoleezza Rice: "We *urgently* need such a Principals level review on the *al Qida* network."[77] Other times, the Principals spurned intelligence or claimed it offered no immediate action, such as the infamous August 2001 President's Daily Brief, "Bin Laden Determined the Strike in US." That brief dismissed outright al Qaeda's intent to hijack U.S. aircraft, calling it "the more sensational threat reporting."[78]

Despite many attempts to pin the blame for the events that were to follow on craven politicians or inept bureaucrats, the fact remains that policy planners, law enforcement authorities, and intelligence officials at every level of the U.S. government failed the American people. A month before the infamous brief, Attorney General John Ashcroft snapped at FBI acting Director Thomas Pickard: "I don't want to hear about al Qaeda anymore."[79] That snap had followed repeated FBI attempts to get Ashcroft's attention on al Qaeda. But in a truly mystifying development, a month later the Justice Department told the media that Ashcroft would be flying exclusively by leased jet aircraft, not commercial, because of a "threat assessment" from the FBI.[80] Neither the FBI nor the Justice Department identified the threat, and left Americans—the primary targets of al Qaeda terrorism—in the dark.

The Post-9/11 Decade

The government often conceals information it thinks may harm U.S. national security. But more often than not, as in the case with 9/11, the government suppresses information it deems potentially embarrassing or incompatible with existing grand strategy. After 9/11, U.S. officials found it politically convenient to conceal disturbing details about private Saudi donors and semiofficial charities that funded bin Laden. America's closest Arab ally had failed to stop the propagation of Salafism and indirect funding of terrorists, much less kill or capture bin Laden before the largest enemy attack on American soil. Past Saudi behavior, and Washington's previous failures, were downplayed and suppressed.

Critics have extensively covered the joint meeting between President Bush and Prince Bandar at the White House on the evening of September 13, 2001,[81] and the permission by a senior U.S. official to allow more than 140 Saudis residing in the United States, including bin Laden family members, to fly on chartered jets and commercial planes immediately following the federal government's grounding of all private flights after 9/11.[82] Points made about those events are valid, but all have been aired before. Far less discussed were the findings of a December 2002 Joint Inquiry by the U.S. Senate and House Intelligence Committees.[83]

Most revealing about the 832-page Joint Inquiry into the U.S. intelligence community's activities before and after 9/11 was what it failed to disclose. The Bush administration redacted virtually an entire 28-page section detailing the role of foreign governments in aiding the 9/11 hijackers. According to one official who read the censored section, it described "very direct, very specific links" between Saudi officials and two of the 9/11 hijackers, links that "cannot be passed off as rogue, isolated or coincidental."[84] Citing a CIA memorandum, the Joint Inquiry referred to "incontrovertible evidence that there is support for these terrorists" from a foreign government; congressional sources said the reference was to Saudi Arabia.[85] Former Florida governor and retired U.S. senator Bob Graham cochaired the Joint Inquiry and claimed unambiguously that the redacted section specified Saudi government assistance to the 9/11 terrorists.[86] "By 'the Saudis,'" Graham later asserted, "I mean the Saudi government and individual Saudis who are for some purposes dependent on the government—which includes all of the elite in the country."[87]

Prince Bandar said before 9/11, "If U.S. security authorities had engaged their Saudi counterparts in a serious and credible manner, in my opinion, we would have avoided what happened."[88] Historical evidence indicates otherwise. "Before 9/11," claimed one CIA source, "the Saudis gave us almost nothing on al Qaeda."[89] Case in point: before 9/11, the CIA asked the Saudis for copies of bin Laden's passport, bank records, and birth certificate. The CIA had still not received the documents after 9/11.[90] Another case was the June 1998 meeting in Kandahar between Prince Turki and the Taliban's Mullah Omar after CIA Director Tenet's visit to the kingdom. Former

Taliban intelligence chief Mohammed Khaksar claimed that, instead of an arrangement to hand over bin Laden, bin Laden agreed not to attack Saudi targets in return for the Saudi government's willingness to provide funds and material assistance to the Taliban—not a demand for bin Laden's extradition or pressure for the closure of al Qaeda training camps.[91]

Yet another case in point: Jordanian intelligence officials who toured Saudi military and security facilities before 9/11 reportedly saw a number of Osama bin Laden screensavers on the office computers of Saudi officials.[92] Indeed, as one CIA source stated after seeing documents and computer files seized from bin Laden operatives, "al Qaeda had the run of Saudi Arabia."[93]

To some observers, Saudi laxity resembled complicity. Bin Laden may have denounced the royal family as an agent of the "Zionist-Crusader alliance" and invoked the liberation of Mecca and Medina from the corrupt hands of the Al Saud family, but decrying the family's self-indulgence as profoundly un-Islamic tells us little about how strongly the Saudis were committed to countering extremists or about the incentives that drove their objectives.

Presumably, private Saudi citizens who knowingly funded al Qaeda sympathized with its cause and remained ideologically committed to bin Laden's worldview. A more charitable explanation, though no less damning, was that Saudis aided al Qaeda in order to inoculate the kingdom from its terrorism. A senior Kuwaiti official would later confirm to America's ambassador in Riyadh about Saudi Defense Minister Prince Sultan bin Abdulaziz Al Saud and Interior Minister Prince Nayef bin Abdulaziz Al Saud, "both had accommodated extremists, in order to keep peace."[94] (Interestingly, in the 1970s the CIA gave Prince Nayef a new desk, which he later discovered contained a listening device.[95]) Similarly, in his 2002 book, *Does America Need a Foreign Policy?* Henry Kissinger said the kingdom "made a tacit bargain with terrorists, so long as terrorist actions were not directed against the host government."[96]

Personal accounts of those connected to bin Laden and his organization also cast doubt on Al Saud claims of financial and emotional distance from bin Laden after his exile from the kingdom. Carmen bin Laden, once married to Osama's half-brother Yeslam, wrote that during the period after bin Laden fled from Sudan to Afghanistan that "Osama, [Yeslam] said, was under the protection of conservative members of the Saudi royal family."[97] In another account, before pleading guilty in 2012 of disclosing classified information, John Kiriakou, the former CIA chief of counterterrorist operations in Pakistan who played a leading role in the 2002 capture of one of bin Laden's top lieutenants, claims he and his CIA colleagues had known for years that elements of Al Saud were funding al Qaeda.[98] Even chief Saudi spokesman and future Saudi Ambassador to Washington Adel Al-Jubeir said that, among the thousands of members of the royal family, a government investigation had uncovered "wrongdoing by some."[99]

The Saudis appeared to try to correct that wrongdoing by getting serious about fighting extremism, especially after al Qaeda's May 2003 attack in Riyadh that killed 36 people and wounded more than 160 others. The government fired 2,000 mosque leaders for voicing support for terrorism, killed hundreds of others, and arrested thousands more. The Ministry of Islamic Affairs issued circulars to clerics and imams encouraging them to reject bigotry in their sermons.[100] Saudi leaders had their work cut out for them. In the immediate aftermath of 9/11, nearly 80 percent of mosques in Saudi Arabia voiced support for bin Laden.[101] And in late 2001, the largest contingent of "enemy combatants" captured by U.S. forces in Afghanistan was Saudi.[102] Even the most well-intentioned government-led campaign to eradicate domestic extremism and redefine Salafism could seemingly be a multigenerational effort.

In Washington, a few observers, mainly neoconservative commentators, made their case against the kingdom in the court of public opinion. *Weekly Standard* editor William Kristol called for deposing the Saudi royal family. In a paper for the Pentagon's Office of Net Assessment, an independent consultant advocated an invasion to secure the kingdom's oil fields. And in a brief to the Defense Policy Board on U.S. policy toward Saudi Arabia, a Rand Corporation analyst proposed targeting the kingdom's oil resources, financial assets, and the holy places of Mecca and Medina.[103] U.S. officials had thought through such issues before during the 1973–1974 OPEC oil embargo, but nothing came of those grandiose plans.[104] In the end, Kristol and other like-minded pundits moved on to mobilize public opinion for war against Iraq's secular dictator, whom the U.S. had fought to keep Iraqi troops off the kingdom's doorstep in the early 1990s.

As the old adage goes, the cover-up can be worse than the crime. After three main justifications for invading Iraq later proved categorically false—Iraq had weapons of mass destruction, Iraq was behind 9/11, and Iraq would welcome foreigners as liberators—White House efforts to focus on Iraq and overlook the kingdom became the subject of widespread speculation.[105] Twenty-one year CIA veteran Robert Baer argued in his 2004 book, *Sleeping with the Devil: How Washington Sold Our Soul for Saudi Crude*, that Washington's cozy ties with Riyadh created a "consent of silence" over the Saudi funding chain for al Qaeda and other violent extremists.[106]

"Consent" indeed. U.S. officials had stated repeatedly that Americans and the world must never forget the terrorist attacks on 9/11. Yet, senior American leaders primarily responsible for shaping U.S. policy toward the kingdom routinely gave their Saudi counterparts the benefit of the doubt—either explaining away the ties between its stateless renegades and the kingdom as coincidental or claiming the Saudis lacked the capability to staunch the flow of terrorist financing.[107] More likely, U.S. policymakers became vested in continuing relations with Riyadh despite other relevant factors.

Other commentary also called the long-standing alliance into question. American journalist Craig Unger detailed the personal and financial connections between the Bush family and the Al Saud monarchy in his *New York Times* bestseller, *House of Bush, House of Saud*. Political commentator and social activist Michael Moore generated significant controversy with his 2004 documentary, *Fahrenheit 9/11*, which argued that the administration's relentless attempt to depict Iraq as America's supreme threat distracted the public from 9/11's real culprits: the Saudis. President Bush was assailed from all sides when critics harped on Unger's and Moore's charges of past and ongoing business and personal relations between the Bush family and the royal family at the helm of an Islamic theocracy. But rather than an explicit cover-up driven by personal allegiances, it was strategic decisions and shared financial, energy, and diplomatic interests that primarily drove Washington's deference to Riyadh; personal connections merely reinforced existing policies.

The Council on Foreign Relations' Middle East Studies Director Rachel Bronson, author of *Thicker Than Oil: America's Uneasy Partnership with Saudi Arabia*, later explained "there is little evidence to suggest that such support has led the Bush family to make decisions at odds with U.S. interests. All previous presidents have sought close relations with the kingdom."[108] Contrary to prevailing assumptions, the fact that previous presidents preserved the U.S.-Saudi alliance, or any alliance for that matter, does not preclude incompetence in Washington. Past presidents' pursuit of close relations with the kingdom does not mean that continuing such support would not harm U.S. interests.

To that point, Pulitzer Prize–winning investigative reporter James Risen—who so accurately detailed CIA activities that the Barack Obama administration served him a subpoena—wrote in a remarkable and revealing passage about Saudi Arabia and the continuing status quo:

> So many people in Washington's power circles—lawyers, and lobbyists, defense contractors, former members of Congress and former White House aides, diplomats and intelligence officers, and even some journalists—rely so heavily on Saudi money or Saudi access that ugly truths about Saudi links to Islamic extremists have been routinely ignored or suppressed.[109]

The revelation of "ugly truths" continued. In June 2004, the U.S. Treasury Department called Al Haramain Islamic Foundation, the largest Saudi-based charity with links to the royal family, "one of the principal Islamic NGOs providing support for the al Qaida network and promoting militant Islamic doctrine worldwide."[110] That September, the U.S. Treasury disclosed that HIF branches in Afghanistan, Albania, Bangladesh, Bosnia, Ethiopia, Indonesia, Kenya, the Netherlands, Pakistan, Somalia, and Tanzania were all providing financial, material, and other operational support to al Qaeda and its affiliates.[111]

Unfortunately, coverage of the war in Iraq excluded these revelations almost entirely from the dominant U.S. media narrative. More exposure to such controversial details may have upset Saudi leaders and sharply reduced Washington's ability to shape policies. But diverting the public's attention to another enemy also perpetuated the public's ignorance about one of the most significant financial sponsors of militant Islamic extremists activities and the alleged necessity of oil security that spurred Washington's unwavering protection of Riyadh.

Despite those developments, the Bush administration's "freedom agenda" reinforced Washington's political engagement in the region. Bush preached the virtues of human liberty and explained how by addressing the "root causes of terrorism" through increased aid for education, democracy promotion, economic cooperation, and development, the United States could plant the seeds of reform. Of course, democratic elections neither diminished the threat of terrorism nor eliminated the underlying grievances that inspired it, as terrorist groups have thrived in free societies, including the Baader-Meinhof Group in West Germany, the Irish Republican Army in Northern Ireland, and the Weather Underground in the United States. Finally, U.S. intelligence agencies monitoring, identifying, and countering Islamic extremism, as detailed in a 2005 Government Accountability Office investigation of U.S. efforts to counter extremism, came to a different conclusion than the White House:

> The Defense Intelligence Agency and other experts agree that the rise in Islamic extremism stems from various factors, including economic stagnation; a disproportionate concentration of population in the 15-to-29-year-old range ("youth bulges"), especially in most Middle Eastern countries; repressive and corrupt governments; and anti-Western sentiments, particularly due to negative perceptions of the United States' foreign policy.[112]

Additionally, an unclassified report by the Pentagon's Defense Science Board commented on the subject of unconditional U.S. support for the Middle East's repressive regimes: "The United States finds itself in the strategically awkward—and potentially dangerous—situation of being the longstanding prop and alliance partner of these authoritarian regimes."[113]

Outside experts agreed. By bolstering tyranny in the Muslim world, a Council on Foreign Relations Independent Task Force argued, U.S. foreign policy strengthened the pull of extremist ideologies that fueled violence against America.[114] Moreover, a Pew Research Center survey stated that support for terrorism was positively correlated with negative views of America.[115] The message was clear: U.S. policies that required the compliance of regimes that oppressed their people were perceived as trying to weaken Islam, not only re-inforcing militant Islamist propaganda, but incentivizing attacks on America.

But like previous American presidents, Bush tolerated despotism in Saudi Arabia. In the deeply conservative kingdom, the Al Saud family monarchy *is* the political system. It owned most print and broadcast media; censored most domestic television and radio out-lets; restricted freedoms of speech, assembly, association, and move-ment; and forbade political parties or similar associations. Bush's oft-repeated warning that "America must confront threats before they fully materialize" overlooked the kingdom's Salafi extremism that threatened freedom. In March 2002, in a horrifying example of how the kingdom's rigid concepts of Islam and social relations could carry life-and-death consequences, its morality police prevented fire-fighters from entering a burning building to rescue female students trapped inside because they were not wearing their head coverings. Fifteen young girls became casualties of strict gender segregation. The head of the Presidency of Girls' Education called the fire "God's will."[116]

Despite the lack of access to accurate information about the threat of Salafi-inspired terrorism, the U.S. policies to counter it were pro-voking further resentment. The declassified judgments of the April 2006 National Intelligence Estimate, which includes input from the country's 16 intelligence agencies, concluded that "the global jihadist movement" was "spreading and adapting," and that activists iden-tifying themselves as jihadists were "increasing in both number and geographic dispersion."[117] That December, the Iraq Study Group, the congressionally mandated assessment of the Iraq war, found that "funding for the Sunni insurgency comes from private individuals within Saudi Arabia and the Gulf States, even as those governments help facilitate U.S. military operations in Iraq by providing basing and overflight rights and by cooperating on intelligence issues."[118]

The perpetual issue of terrorist financing offers an excellent case study of inconsistency in the conduct of foreign policy. To stem the flow of private Saudi funds to terrorists, the Riyadh government issued numerous decrees and created new institutions to increase government supervision over charitable donations. It removed col-lection boxes in shopping malls, prohibited cash contributions at mosques, and adopted new restrictions on the banking activities of Saudi-based charities.[119] "The Saudis are now arguably our most important counterterrorism intelligence partner," wrote David Rundell, the U.S. deputy chief of mission in Riyadh, in April 2009.[120] But U.S.-Saudi intelligence sharing and cooperation also depended upon senior-level American leaders communicating the U.S. government's counterterrorism priorities and fostering among their Saudi counterparts the necessary political will to address the problem of terrorist financing. On that score, the results were indisputably negative.

"Still, donors in Saudi Arabia constitute the most significant source of funding to Sunni terrorist groups worldwide,"[121] wrote Secretary of State Hillary Clinton in a December 2009 diplomatic cable to U.S. Embassies in Riyadh, Kuwait, Abu Dhabi, Doha, and Islamabad. "Saudi Arabia," Clinton continued, "remains a critical financial support base for al-Qa'ida, the Taliban, LeT, and other terrorist groups, including Hamas."[122] Despite important progress in combating terrorism, particularly in investigating and detaining financial facilitators, Saudi seriousness about combating extremists inside the kingdom was seemingly limited when it came to preventing extremists' permeation abroad.[123] That same year, U.S. State and Treasury Department officials found that, despite Saudi restrictions regarding funds, multilateral charitable organizations still operate "largely outside of the strict Saudi restrictions covering domestic charities."[124]

In these circumstances, two widely circulated images encapsulated criticism of America's subservience to the monarchy: one in 2005 of President Bush holding hands with and giving a ceremonial kiss to then Crown Prince Abdullah at the Crawford ranch, which struck many observers as symbolically inappropriate; and one in 2009 of President Barack Obama bowing to King Abdullah at the G20 summit in London, which ignited a media uproar. But despite the mutual admiration, old problems have resurfaced in the U.S.-Saudi alliance.

Arab Sunni Ally, Persian Shiite Enemy

"Thank God for bringing Obama to the presidency," Saudi Arabia's King Abdullah gushed to U.S. officials in 2009.[125] Such high hopes faded fast. In 2010, the pro-democracy research institute Freedom House reported a net decline in liberty across the world for the fifth consecutive year.[126] President Bush's Freedom Agenda and

President Obama's attempts to revive it coincided with the longest continual decline of political and civil rights in the institute's four decades of recordkeeping. Meanwhile, America's image around the world had plummeted to record lows, along with perceptions of its moral leadership, following revelations of torture and violations of human rights, targeted killings, indefinite detention, and preventive invasion. The world perceived the United States as unconstrained by the rules and values it imposed upon others; soon, it appeared to retreat from its oft-stated claim to oppose policies that subvert human freedom.

In January 2011, American leaders faced a serious moral challenge when authoritarian allies across North Africa and the Middle East violently suppressed public demonstrations known as the Arab Spring. The uprisings sent Tunisia's President Zine El Abidine Ben Ali into exile in Saudi Arabia and Egypt's Hosni Mubarak to a presidential palace in the Red Sea resort of Sharm el-Sheikh. Critics contended that the Saudis saw the Obama administration as a threat to their domestic security, as the Saudis had wanted aggressive U.S. measures to retain the regional status quo. Obama's failure to do so showed either that he discarded America's long-standing policy or that he lacked the capability to protect those allies from their own people.[127] Some alleged that regional upheavals had put the allies "on a collision course."[128]

In actuality, the Obama administration, much like its predecessors, projected the image that it attempted to balance American interests with ideals. Yet, it continued to back execrable Arab regimes. Only when such support proved intolerable to continue did the administration present itself as a consummate protector of human freedom, then proceeding to support new rulers that abandoned revolution in order to reinstate the principal features of its previous regime.

Moreover, far from peaceful protests, the Saudis saw behind the Arab Spring an Iranian-backed strategy to subvert Arab Sunni states. A year before the Arab Spring, U.S. diplomats reported that senior Saudi leaders "have been openly critical of U.S. policies they describe as having shifted the regional balance of power in favor of arch-rival Iran."[129] Those "U.S. policies" included the invasion and occupation of Iraq, which knocked off Saddam Hussein; Iraq was, until then, Persian Shia Iran's primary foe. Thereafter, Washington and Riyadh explicitly strove to contain Iranian influence and thwart its nuclear capabilities (explained in detail below). To senior Saudi leaders, the nuclear issue also symbolized Iran's drive for regional supremacy, and Riyadh encouraged Gulf countries to consider stationing nuclear weapons as a deterrent.[130]

With political values at cross purposes and decades of U.S.–Middle East doctrine unraveling, Washington scored an indisputable foreign policy achievement. On May 1, 2011, President Obama announced that U.S. Special Forces had entered northern Pakistan and killed Osama bin Laden. That essential U.S. objective deprived extremists of an iconic figure. But the greatest tragedy of the post-9/11 experience was that the war on terror could never be truly "won." Threats continued. That December, the Philippine and Indonesian offices of Saudi-based charity International Islamic Relief Organization came under international scrutiny for actively providing assistance to al Qaeda.[131]

Beyond organizations and established charities, the more insidious threat came from terrorism's inherent fragmentation. The uncontrollable spread of Salafist ideology continued to turn disenchanted young Muslims into hardened militants. Documents recovered from bin Laden's compound found that he appeared to lack an organized system to direct worldwide operations. In fact, bin Laden and other senior leaders of al Qaeda central wanted stunning attacks against America and its allies and disdained al Qaeda affiliates that promoted independent, lone-wolf attacks. One such affiliate was al Qaeda in the Arabian Peninsula (AQAP) and its local propagandist, Anwar al-Awlaki. The American-born and raised Al-Awlaki used reasoned arguments similar to bin Laden's, but he used social media and AQAP's English-language Web-based publication *Inspire* to promote violence, strict adherence to religious devotion, and belief in a worldwide Islamic caliphate.[132]

On April 15, 2013, Tamerlan and Dzhokhar Tsarnaev, two ethnic Chechen brothers, set off pressure-cooker bombs at the finish line of the Boston Marathon, killing 3 people, maiming 200 others, and severing the limbs of over a half-dozen blast victims. Preliminary investigations showed no connection to international terrorism but suggested the brothers were influenced by the Saudi-inspired Salafist concept of an international Islamic caliphate. The social media account of the younger Tsarnaev linked to Salafist videos and referenced Islamist insurgents in Russia's rebellious North Caucasus, including the Muslim republics of Dagestan and Chechnya.[133] Friends of the elder Tsarnaev, who attended a mosque attended by Salafists while in Dagestan, say he grew to oppose Western sensibilities and customs and regularly read militant Islamist propaganda, including AQAP's *Inspire*.[134] Interestingly, after the Cold War, Saudi Arabia had sent millions of Qurans to post-Soviet Central Asian republics for their large Muslim populations.[135] And, in the 1990s, many young Muslims from Dagestan traveled to the kingdom to study.

The legacy of the unintended consequences of Saudi Salafism arose once again in shaping the Middle East's political transformation. In elections held in the post–Arab Spring Middle East, ultra-conservative Salafists formed political parties and factions in Algeria, Bahrain, Kuwait, Libya, and Yemen and won pluralities in Tunisia, Egypt, and Morocco.[136] Salafists rejected minority and women's rights, restricted personal and political liberties, and opposed the secular interests and values of Western societies. In its competition for religious and regional dominance with Iran, the Sunni Arab kingdom continued aggressive policies directly and by proxy across the region.

Amid fears of Iranian encirclement, the Arab kingdom backed Salafists who challenged what Jordan's King Abdullah called the "Shiite Crescent," the arc of Shiite brethren and influence spanning Iran, Iraq, Bahrain, Lebanon, Syria, Saudi Arabia's Eastern Province, and elsewhere. In Bahrain, for instance, home to a major U.S. naval base for the U.S. Fifth Fleet, the Saudis had sent troops in March 2011 to support the Al-Khalifa ruling family of Bahrain and its privileged Arab Sunni minority and to crush peaceful protests among the country's disadvantaged Shiite majority. The United States colluded with a Saudi police state that not only denied its own subjects political and personal freedoms, but also obstructed regional progress.

"At its core," said commentator Hazem Amin, who in October 2013 believed Syrian Salafists were increasingly embracing radical views close to al Qaeda, "the new Syrian Salafism is jihadist in nature. It is moving towards extremism."[137] Washington refused to abide by the policies of its oil-rich ally, particularly in Syria, where U.S.-Saudi interests genuinely diverged. Saudi Arabia, along with Qatar, furnished weapons and other supplies to well-organized rebel Sunni and Salafi militant groups to fight against Syrian dictator Bashar Al-Assad and his minority Alawites, a small Shiite sect, that were allied with Shiite Iran and Lebanon's Shiite political-terrorist group, Hezbollah.[138] Saudi and Qatari funding to their "Salafi Crescent" turned Syria's civil war into a terror attraction and a reflection of the region's intra-Islamic turmoil. Militants attracted young, middle-class Australians, Canadians, Americans, Germans, French, and other aspiring jihadists—a virtual cornucopia of terrorism. Militants flocked to join the rebel cause and seek martyrdom, including those formerly fighting U.S. and coalition forces in Iraq.

Although the United States later sold $640 million worth of U.S.-made cluster bombs to Saudi Arabia, despite their ban by 83 countries and the U.S. State Department's admission of "international concern," the partners began to vent their differences publicly and pursue policies without consultation.[139] In August 2013, after Syrian opposition groups claimed Assad used chemical weapons, President Obama appeared to back away from his earlier "red line" vow to take military action against Assad if the Syrian dictator used chemical weapons against his own people. With some noticeable reluctance, Obama turned to Congress for approval of missile strikes, thereby putting his own policy prescription at risk. In response, Ahmed al-Ibrahahim, an adviser to some of the kingdom's royals and officials, claimed Obama had "lost credibility after Syria."[140] He continued: "The bond of trust between America and Saudi Arabia has been broken in the Obama years. . . . We feel we have been stabbed in the back by Obama." Prince Turki followed by calling the president's approach to Syria "lamentable."

In reality, America's longtime Arab ally was finally forced to pay the price for the violence, repression, and bloodshed its policies had inflicted at home and spread overseas. Far from constituting a vital component of U.S. national security, the Saudi government was supporting militant Islamist extremists and funding the propagation of worldviews that threatened U.S. political interests and the secular values of Western societies. Indeed, years before on Capitol Hill, on the subject of Afghanistan and Pakistan that applies equally to events in Syria, Secretary Clinton was remarkably frank about past U.S. government policies:

> I mean, let's remember here, the people we are fighting today, we funded 20 years ago. And we did it because we were locked in this struggle with the Soviet Union. . . . And it was President Reagan, in partnership

with the Congress, led by Democrats, who said you know what, it sounds like a pretty good idea. Let's deal with the ISI and the Pakistani military and let's go recruit these Mujahedeen and that's great. Let's get some to come from Saudi Arabia and other places, importing their Wahabi [sic] brand of Islam so that we can go beat the Soviet Union. And guess what? They retreated. They lost billions of dollars and it led to the collapse of the Soviet Union. So there's . . . a very strong argument, which is it wasn't a bad investment to end the Soviet Union, *but let's be careful what we sow, because we will harvest.*[141]

Alliance commitments have the tendency to push American leaders to adopt policies they might not otherwise take. This time, when Saudi and American proponents of overthrowing Assad called for deeper U.S. involvement, they faced fierce resistance from Congress and the public. After more than a decade, with more than 8,000 Americans dead; 40,000 wounded and traumatized; $4 trillion spent, with the meter still running; sectarian chaos; and al Qaeda, ISIS, and other militant cells active in Iraq, Libya, Pakistan, Yemen, Somalia, and Syria, it appears that the war on terror's tumultuous aftermath hardened the public's cynicism about becoming entrapped yet again in a region where anti-Western hatreds run deep. Ironically, Riyadh's incessant proselytizing bred much of the hatred that prompted Washington's reluctance to become more involved.

Conclusion

Although Saudi Arabia has played a major role on many issues of critical importance to the United States, and the kingdom's wealth and influence accords it considerable clout in Washington, it is impossible to have an informed debate about that pivotal alliance when key factual questions surrounding it remain unanswered. Before and after 9/11, American leaders whitewashed the conduct of private Saudi-based donors and charities that funded bin Laden's movement and the affiliates who fought under its flag. In the course of forgiving irredeemable behavior, U.S. leaders engaged in their own: downplaying their responsibility for doing too little to stop those offenses, misleading the public with clumsy attempts to cast suspicion upon Iraq, and supporting an ally that continued to sponsor Salafist insurgencies and spread sectarianism through intra-Islamic civil wars. Even after Washington stood by Riyadh, the Saudi regime raised objections to Washington for expanding Shiite Iranian influence by overthrowing Iraq's Sunni Arab dictator and for refusing to crush revolutions during the Arab Spring. Decades of collaboration had bred a false sense of entitlement.

Shortly after the 2011 revolutionary upheavals swept the region, many aspects of the alliance also began to transform. Former U.S. Ambassador to Saudi Arabia Chas Freeman recounted a comment made by King Abdullah, then crown prince, on the kingdom and theme of Salafism that "a friend who does not help you is no better than an enemy who does you no harm." Freeman explained that the "automaticity of friendship, a willingness to go out of your way to do things notwithstanding the absence of any interest of your own is gone."[142] Moreover, on the subject of oil, Saudi Arabia's inability to bring new supply for a sustained period of time, combined with its domestic energy consumption used to quell internal political unrest, and impressive new developments in the U.S. energy sector, means that the relevance of Saudi oil to America became greatly diminished.[143]

Given these and other changing dynamics, the United States must govern its future policies toward the kingdom based upon legitimate disagreements and genuine constraints, not slavish attempts to promote a flawed alliance through pervasive misinformation. With Saudi Arabia, as with Pakistan, American leaders must ensure that its allies make concerted efforts against militants at home *and* abroad. If allies fail to move against militants or their funding sources quickly enough, U.S. leaders should not hesitate to take action themselves. Moreover, after tragedies like 9/11, U.S. officials must be willing to censure the Saudis and redefine the parameters of America's security commitment.

Finally, a richer public dialogue about terrorism, its sources, and its consequences could have helped the American public make better decisions about U.S. involvement in the Middle East and allowed for a wider range of policy choices. Without that knowledge, the public cannot know what policies to avoid repeating. To the extent that U.S. officials keep the public in the dark, the public will continue to be critically endangered for it.

Notes

Introduction

1. Tom Barnes, "Jamal Khashoggi: Pompeo All Smiles in Meeting with Saudi Crown Prince Mohammed bin Salman over Journalist Disappearance," *Independent*, October 18, 2018, https://www.independent.co.uk/news/world/middle-east/jamal-khashoggi-mike-pompeo-saudi-arabia-mohammed-bin-salman-saudi-arabia-mbs-murder-a8589576.html.

2. Peter Baker, "In Trump's Saudi Bargain, the Bottom Line Proudly Wins Out," *New York Times*, October 14, 2018, https://www.nytimes.com/2018/10/14/us/politics/trump-saudi-arabia-arms-deal.html.

3. Mark Townsend, "Sheikh Nimr al-Nimr: Shia Cleric Was a Thorn in Saudi Regime's Side," *Guardian*, January 2, 2016, https://www.theguardian.com/world/2016/jan/02/sheikh-nimr-al-nimr-shia-cleric-thorn-saudi-regime-side.

4. Krishnadev Calamur, "Saudi Arabia Rejects Human-Rights Criticism, Then Crucifies Someone," *Atlantic*, August 9, 2018, https://www.theatlantic.com/international/archive/2018/08/saudi-crucifixion/567128/.

5. Amnesty International, "Saudi Arabia 2017/2018," https://www.amnesty.org/en/countries/middle-east-and-north-africa/saudi-arabia/report-saudi-arabia/.

6. Daniel Larison, "The U.S. Enables and Indulges Saudi War Crimes," *American Conservative*, August 14, 2018, https://www.theamericanconservative.com/larison/the-u-s-enables-and-indulges-saudi-war-crimes/.

7. Agence France-Presse, "'Killing A Generation': One Million More Children at Risk from Famine in Yemen," *Guardian*, September 18, 2018, https://www.theguardian.com/world/2018/sep/19/yemen-famine-million-more-children-at-risk-; Kate Lyons, "Yemen's Cholera Outbreak Now the Worst in History as Millionth Case Looms," *Guardian*, October 12, 2017, https://www.theguardian.com/global-development/2017/oct/12/yemen-cholera-outbreak-worst-in-history-1-million-cases-by-end-of-year.

8. "HRW Wants End to Saudi Arms Sale after Yemen School Bus Attack," *Al Jazeera*, September 2, 2018, https://www.aljazeera.com/news/2018/09/hrw-saudi-arms-sale-yemen-school-bus-attack-180902075014341.html.

9. Jonathan Landay, "Pompeo Says Saudi, UAE Trying to Avoid Civilian Harm in Yemen," Reuters, September 12, 2018, https://www.reuters.com/article/us-yemen-security-usa/saudi-uae-trying-to-avoid-civilian-harm-in-yemen-pompeo-idUSKCN1LS1XR.

10. Daniel Larison, "The U.S. Is Deeply Complicit in Saudi Coalition Crimes in Yemen," *American Conservative*, August 13, 2018, https://www.theamericanconservative.com/larison/the-u-s-is-deeply-complicit-in-saudi-coalition-crimes-in-yemen/.

11. Thomas Juneau, "No, Yemen's Houthis Actually Aren't Iranian Puppets," *Washington Post*, May 16, 2016, https://www.washingtonpost.com/news/monkey-cage/wp/2016/05/16/contrary-to-popular-belief-houthis-arent-iranian-proxies/?noredirect=on&utm_term=.9c61e74012e6.

12. "Al Qaeda Appeals for Help to Repel Houthis in Central Yemen," Reuters, March 9, 2017, https://www.reuters.com/article/us-yemen-security/al-qaeda-appeals-for-help-to-repel-houthis-in-central-yemen-idUSKBN16G2X3.

13. Ted Galen Carpenter, "Why America Must Put Interests before Ideals," *American Conservative*, August 15, 2018, https://www.theamericanconservative.com/articles/why-america-must-put-interests-before-ideals/?mc_cid=60252a31bd&mc_eid=a6aa34c728.

14. Henry Kissinger, "Reflections on Containment," *Foreign Affairs* 73, No. 3 (June 1994): 130. https://www.foreignaffairs.com/articles/1994-05-01/reflections-containment.

15. Ted Galen Carpenter and Malou Innocent, *Perilous Partners: The Benefits and Pitfalls of America's Alliances with Authoritarian Regimes* (Washington: Cato Institute, 2015), 137–78; 397–426.

16. Carpenter and Innocent, *Perilous Partners*, 399-401.

17. Charles Lister, *The Syrian Jihad: Al-Qaeda, the Islamic State and the Evolution of an Insurgency* (Oxford, UK: Oxford University Press, 2016); Christopher Phillips, *The Battle for Syria: International Rivalry in the New Middle East* (New Haven, CT: Yale University Press, 2016).

18. Ted Galen Carpenter, *Gullible Superpower: U.S. Support for Bogus Foreign Democratic Movements,* (Washington: Cato Institute, 2019).

19. Emma Ashford and John Glaser, "Unforced Error: The Risks of Confrontation with Iran," Cato Institute Policy Analysis no. 822, October 9, 2017; Emma Ashford, "Kill the Iran Deal, Open Pandora's Box," Cato-at-Liberty, May 8, 2018, https://www.cato.org/blog/killing-jcpoa-opens-pandoras-box; and John Glaser, "Trump Leans on Distortions to Explain Iran Deal Withdrawal," Axios, May 9, 2018, https://www.cato.org/publications/commentary/trump-leans-distortions-explain-iran-deal-withdrawal.

20. Ted Galen Carpenter, "Is Washington Backing the Wrong Side in the Iranian-Saudi Regional Feud," *National Interest,* June 10, 2017, https://nationalinterest.org/blog/the-skeptics/washington-backing-the-wrong-side-the-iranian-saudi-regional-21092.

21. Emma Ashford, "Don't Believe Donald Trump; We'll Be Just Fine without Saudi Arabia," *USA Today*, October 16, 2018, https://www.usatoday.com/story/opinion/2018/10/16/donald-trump-well-fine-without-saudi-arabia-talker/1657822002/.

Chapter 1

1. For a history of the Arabian Peninsula and Saudi Wahhabism, see Alexei Vassiliev, *The History of Saudi Arabia* (New York: New York University Press, 2000).

2. Cairo's al-Azhar and Sunni scholars at other centers of Islamic learning dismissed Abd al-Wahhab's teachings, criticizing them as uncompromising and dismissing their permissibility of warfare against fellow Muslims. Hamid Algar, *Wahhabism: A Critical Essay* (Oneota, NY: Islamic Publications International, 2002); and Vassiliev, *The History of Saudi Arabia*, pp. 64–82.

3. King Abd al-Aziz bin Abd al-Rahman al-Saud.

4. John A. DeNovo, *American Interests and Policies in the Middle East, 1900–1939* (Minneapolis: University of Minnesota Press, 1963), pp. 167–209; Daniel Yergin, *The Prize: The Epic Quest for Oil, Money, & Power* (New York: Simon & Schuster, 1991), pp. 298–300.

5. Anthony Cave Brown, *Oil, God, and Gold: The Story of Aramco and the Saudi Kings* (New York: Houghton Mifflin, 1999), p. 52.

6. Chas W. Freeman Jr., *America's Misadventures in the Middle East* (Charlottesville, VA: Just World Books, 2010), p. 201n.

7. Joshua Teitelbaum, "Holier Than Thou: Saudi Arabia's Islamic Opposition," Washington Institute for Near East Policy, Policy Paper No. 52, November 1, 2000; Tim Niblock, ed., *State, Society, and Economy in Saudi Arabia* (New York: St. Martin's Press, 1981); and Anthony H. Cordesman and Nawaf Obaid, *National Security in Saudi Arabia: Threats, Responses, and Challenges* (Westport, CT: Praeger, 2005), p. 391.

8. Despite signing a treaty with King Ibn Saud on May 20, 1927, the British sided later with the Hashemites for their loyalty and compliance with British interests. See Timothy J. Paris, *Britain, the Hashemites, and Arab Rule, 1920–1925: The Sherifian Solution* (London: Routledge, 2003); and Nadav Safran, *Saudi Arabia: The Ceaseless Quest for Security* (Ithaca, NY: Cornell University Press, 1988), pp. 64–67.

9. Parker T. Hart, *Saudi Arabia and the United States: Birth of a Security Partnership* (Bloomington, IN: Indiana University Press, 1998), p. 38.

10. In April 1941, Moffett explained that the king could not hold on to his dominion with only the fees from the annual pilgrimage to Mecca (*hajj*). He encouraged Roosevelt to advance the king $6 million annually for five years against the value of oil to be purchased by Washington. See "Mr. James A. Moffett to President Roosevelt," April 16, 1941, in *Foreign Relations of the United States* 1941 (hereafter, *FRUS*), vol. III, pp. 624–25; see also Hart, *Saudi Arabia and the United States*, p. 29. Rodgers's push came in February 1943. See "Multinational Oil Corporations and U.S. Foreign Policy," Report by U.S. Senate Committee on Foreign Relations, Subcommittee on Multinational Corporations, 93rd Cong., 1st sess., http://www.mtholyoke.edu/acad/intrel/oil1.htm.

11. Michael A. Bernstein, *The Great Depression: Delayed Recovery and Economic Change in America, 1929–1939* (Cambridge: Cambridge University Press, 1987), pp. 201–2.

12. "President Roosevelt to the Lend-Lease Administrator (Stettinius)," February 18, 1943, *FRUS* 1943, vol. IV, The Near East and Africa (Washington: Government Printing Office, 1943), p. 859, http://digicoll.library.wisc.edu/cgi-bin/FRUS/FRUS -idx?type=header&id=FRUS.FRUS1943v04; and Yergin, *The Prize*, p. 397.

13. For an analysis of why U.S.-Saudi relations were not always about oil, see Rachel Bronson, *Thicker than Oil: America's Uneasy Partnership with Saudi Arabia* (New York: Oxford University Press, 2006). According to William A. Eddy, the future U.S. Consul General in Dhahran, an account of the meeting contained no specific reference to agreements or commitments by the United States or by Saudi Arabia. See William A. Eddy, *F.D.R. Meets Ibn Saud*, repr. (Vista, CA: Selwa Press, 2005), http://www .susris.com/documents/2010/100222-fdr-abdulaziz-eddy.pdf.

14. "Draft Memorandum to President Truman," [n.d.], U.S. Political and Economic Policies [Annex], Prepared by the Chief of the Division of Near Eastern Affairs (Merriam) and to the Director of the Office of Near Eastern and African Affairs (Henderson) in early August 1945, *FRUS* 1945, vol. VIII, The Near East and Africa, p. 45, http://images.library.wisc.edu/FRUS/EFacs/1945v08/reference/frus .frus1945v08.i0013.pdf.

15. Central Intelligence Agency, "The Current Situation in the Mediterranean and the Near East," October 17, 1947. Truman Papers, PSF, Box 254. The CIA was primarily concerned with Iran, Turkey, Egypt, French North Africa, Libya, and Spain.

16. Robert Vitalis, *America's Kingdom: Mythmaking on the Saudi Oil Frontier* (Palo Alto, CA: Stanford University Press, 2009), p. 81. Memorandum from Under Secretary of the Navy to Acting Secretary of State, [n.d.], with attached Memorandum for the President, June 26, 1945, RG 59, F.245/6-2645.

17. "The Secretary of Defense (Forrestal) to Secretary of State," November 8, 1948, *FRUS* 1948, vol. V, p. 252. See also C. L. Sulzberger, "Saudi Arabia Base Key U.S. Airfield," *New York Times*, November 24, 1946.

18. For more on how the State Department under President Truman helped U.S. oil policy secure increased markets and additional sources of supply, see Michael James Lacey, ed., *The Truman Presidency* (New York: Cambridge University Press, 1989). A number of influential thinkers believed private corporations were complements to government. A perceptive law-review essay published in 1960 explored the legal and foreign policy ramifications of calling the corporation a "government" and the dominance this thinking had in the pre- and postwar years regarding oil. See Arthur S. Miller, "The Corporation as a Private Government in the World Community," *Virginia Law Review* 46, no. 8 (December 1960): 1551.

19. James R. Ralph Jr., "*U.S. Middle East Oil: The Petroleum Reserves Corporation* (Carlisle Barracks, PA: U.S. Army War College, 1972); Aaron David Miller, *Search for Security: Saudi Arabian Oil and American Foreign Policy, 1939–1949* (Chapel Hill: University of North Carolina Press, 1991), pp. 68–71, 92–97; and Michael B. Stoff, *Oil, War, and American Security: The Search for a National Policy on Foreign Oil, 1941–1947* (New Haven, CT: Yale University Press, 1980), pp. 41–46, 58–61. King Ibn Saud was reportedly "astonished and annoyed" by the ultimatums. See Douglas Little, "Pipeline Politics: America, TAPLINE, and the Arabs," *Business History Review* 64 (Summer 1990): 270.

20. Miles Copeland, *The Game of Nations: The Amorality of Power Politics* (New York: Simon & Schuster, 1969), pp. 44–45.

21. That account and those from others are verified by other evidence. See Andrew Rathmell, "Copeland and Za'im: Re-evaluating the Evidence," *Intelligence and National Security* 11, no. 1 (January 1996): 89–105; Andrew Rathmell, *Secret War in the Middle East: The Covert Struggle for Syria, 1949–1961* (New York: I.B. Tauris Academic Studies, 1995); Douglas Little, "Cold War and Covert Action: The United States and Syria, 1945–1958," *Middle East Journal* 44 (Winter 1990): 55–57; and Douglas Little, "Pipeline Politics: America, TAPLINE, and the Arabs," *Business History Review* 64 (Summer 1990): 277–81. For Copeland quote, see *The Game of Nations*, p. 50.

22. The State Department also said that "other matters involving security were tied up in this relationship." Quoted in Miller, "The Corporation as a Private Government in the World Community," pp. 1546–47.

23. "President Truman to King Abdul Aziz Ibn Saud of Saudi Arabia," *FRUS* 1950, vol. V, October 31, 1950, pp. 1190–91, http://images.library.wisc.edu/FRUS/EFacs/1950v05/reference/frus.frus1950v05.i0014.pdf; "Memorandum by the Central Intelligence Agency," September 24, 1951, *FRUS* 1951, vol. I, National Security Affairs: Foreign Economic Policy, pp. 205–6.

24. Copeland, *The Game of Nations*, p. 58.

25. "Letter from William A. Eddy to Dorothy Thompson" [Christian-Muslim Anticommunist Propaganda Theme], June 7, 1951. National Archives. Record Group 59. Records of the Department of State. Lot Files. 57 D 298, http://www.gwu.edu/~nsarchiv/NSAEBB/NSAEBB78/propaganda%20026.pdf.

26. Ian Johnson, *A Mosque in Munich: Nazis, the CIA, and the Rise of the Muslim Brotherhood in the West* (New York: Houghton Mifflin Harcourt, 2010), pp. 41, 69.

27. After 1959, the U.S. Military and Advisory Group (MAAG) was known as the U.S. Military Training Mission (USMTM). For more on formal U.S.-Saudi security relations, and MAAG and USMTM, see David E. Long, *The United States and*

Saudi Arabia: Ambivalent Allies (Boulder, CO: Westview Press, 1985), p. 35; and Brown, *Oil, God, and Gold*, p. 261.

28. U.S. intelligence had penetrated the Brotherhood during WWII, learning its leadership and activities. On Rida, see Dore Gold, *Hatred's Kingdom: How Saudi Arabia Supports the New Global Terrorism* (Washington: Regnery Publishing, 2003), pp. 54–55.

29. Kai Bird, *Crossing Mandelbaum Gate: Coming of Age between the Arabs and Israelis, 1956–1978* (New York: Scribner, 2010), p. 195.

30. For details of the visit, see Johnson, *A Mosque in Munich*, pp. 116–19.

31. Jefferson Caffery, U.S. Department of State, "Colloquium on Islamic Culture and Saeed Ramadan," Foreign Service Dispatch, National Security Archive, July 27, 1953, http://www.gwu.edu/~nsarchiv/NSAEBB/NSAEBB78/propaganda%20103.pdf. The CIA front organization was the Institute for the Study of the USSR in Munich. See Johnson, *A Mosque in Munich*, pp. 133–34.

32. Department of State, memorandum from Wilson S. Compton to David K. E. Bruce, "Colloquium on Islamic Culture to Be Held in September, 1953, under the Joint Sponsorship of the Library of Congress and Princeton University" [Attached to cover note dated January 16, 1953; includes enclosure], January 13, 1953, National Archives. Record Group 59. Records of the Department of State. Decimal Files, 1950–1954, http://www.gwu.edu/~nsarchiv/NSAEBB/NSAEBB78/propaganda%20089.pdf; http://www.archives.gov/research/guide-fed-records/groups/306.html#306.1.

33. Johnson, *A Mosque in Munich*, p. 117.

34. U.S. Assistant Secretary of State for Near Eastern Affairs William Rountree emphasized that poor nations provided fertile fields for anti-U.S. propaganda. "441. Memorandum of a Conversation, Department of State, Washington, November 26, 1956," Department of State, Central Files, 611.87/11–2656. Secret. Drafted by Newsom, http://history.state.gov/historicaldocuments/frus1955-57v12/d441. For NATO findings, see "Report by the Council Deputies to the North Atlantic Council: Soviet Foreign Policy," Conference files, lot 59 D 95, CF 104, Top Secret. February 6, 1952, *FRUS, 1952–1954*, vol. V, pp. 280–85.

35. Saud bin Abdul Aziz.

36. For more on propaganda operations, see "Memorandum on the Substance of Discussions at the Department of State-Joint Chiefs of Staff Meeting, Pentagon, Washington, May 23, 1956, 11:30 a.m.," Department of State, State-JCS Meetings: Lot 61 D 417(Top Secret), http://images.library.wisc.edu/FRUS/EFacs2/1955-57v12/reference/frus.frus195557v12.i0008.pdf. The CIA eventually severed the cozy ties between Nasser and Saud, convincing the latter that Saudi money for Egyptian propaganda was assisting communists. See Copeland, *The Game of Nations*, pp. 245–46. Beforehand, though, after proclaiming the need for closer Arab and Islamic ties and opposition to the Baghdad Pact, King Saud concluded a defense pact with Egypt in October 1955 and a similar pact with Syria in March. See Vassiliev, *The History of Saudi Arabia*, pp. 338–53.

37. On the rich history of Zionism in America, see Peter Grose, *Israel in the Mind of America* (New York: Schocken-Random House, 1984). On American sympathy for the Jewish people and its impact on politics, see Aaron Berman, *Nazism, the Jews, and American Zionism, 1933–1948* (Detroit: Wayne State University Press, 1990); and David H. Shapiro, *From Philanthropy to Activism: The Political Transformation of American Zionism in the Holocaust Years, 1933–1945* (New York: Pergamon Press, 1994). Also see Michelle Mart, *Eye on Israel: How America Came to View Israel as an Ally* (Albany: State University of New York Press, 2006), pp. 73, 76; Peter L. Hahn, *Crisis and Crossfire:*

The United States and the Middle East Since 1945 (Washington: Potomac Books Inc., 2005); Paul Boyer, *When Time Shall Be No More: Prophecy Belief in Modern American Culture* (Cambridge, MA: Harvard University Press, 1992); and Yaakov Ariel, *On Behalf of Israel: American Fundamentalist Attitudes toward Jews, Judaism, and Zionism, 1865–1945* (Brooklyn: Carlson, 1991).

38. For excellent accounts of U.S. national security issues in the Middle East in the decade after World War II, see John C. Campbell, *Defense of the Middle East: Problems of American Policy* (New York: HarperCollins, 1958); and Melvin P. Leffler, *A Preponderance of Power: National Security, the Truman Administration, and the Cold War* (Palo Alto: Stanford University Press, 1992).

39. "Joseph Grew to Harry S. Truman," May 1, 1945, President's Secretary's Files, Truman Papers, Harry S. Truman Library and Museum, http://www.trumanlibrary .org/whistlestop/study_collections/israel/large/documents/newPDF/2-6.pdf; "Edward Stettinius to Harry S. Truman," April 18, 1945, President's Secretary's Files, Truman Papers, Harry S. Truman Library and Museum, http://www.trumanlibrary .org/whistlestop/study_collections/israel/large/documents/newPDF/2-5.pdf; "Joint Chiefs of Staff to State-War-Navy Coordinating Committee," June 21, 1946, President's Secretary's Files, Truman Papers, Harry S. Truman Library and Museum, http://www.trumanlibrary.org/whistlestop/study_collections/israel/large /documents/newPDF/2-14.pdf; "Correspondence between William L. Clayton and Harry S. Truman," September 12, 1946, President's Secretary's Files, Truman Papers, Harry S. Truman Library and Museum, http://www.trumanlibrary.org/whistlestop /study_collections/israel/large/documents/newPDF/72.pdf.

40. PPS 19, "Report by the Policy Planning Staff on Position of the United States with Respect to Palestine," January 19, 1948, *FRUS* 1948, vol. V, part 2, p. 552, http:// digital.library.wisc.edu/1711.dl/FRUS.FRUS1948v05p2.

41. Dwight D. Eisenhower, *The White House Years: Waging Peace, 1956–1961* (New York: Doubleday, 1965), p. 114.

42. "Excerpts from Dulles Testimony to Senators on Arms Shipments to Middle East," *New York Times,* February 26, 1956.

43. See Henry J. Epstein, *American Jewish Congress v. Elmer A. Carter et al.,* 19 Misc. 2d 205 (July 15, 1959), http://ny.findacase.com/research/wfrmDocViewer .aspx/xq/fac.19590715_0044738.NY.htm/qx.

44. Eisenhower resorted to flashing lights and military police for the monarch. Wilbur Crane Eveland, *Ropes of Sand: America's Failure in the Middle East* (New York: W.W. Norton, 1980), p. 242.

45. Eisenhower, *Waging Peace,* p. 190.

46. Lawrence Wright, *The Looming Tower: Al-Qaeda and the Road to 9/11* (New York: Knopf, 2006), p. 147; and Carmen bin Laden, *Inside the Kingdom: My Life in Saudi Arabia* (New York: Grand Central Publishing, 2005).

47. Copeland, *The Game of Nations,* pp. 246–47.

48. "226. Diary Entry by the President," March 28, 1956, Eisenhower Library, Whitman File, Eisenhower Diaries. Top Secret. *FRUS* 1955–1957, vol. XV, Arab-Israeli Dispute, January 1–July 1956, doc. 226, http://history.state.gov/historicaldocuments /frus1955-57v15/d226; "Memorandum of Discussion at the 260th Meeting of NSC, October 6, 1955," *FRUS* 1955–1957, vol. XIII, Eisenhower Library, Whitman File, NSC Records (Top Secret; Eyes Only), Drafted by Gleason on October 7. http://images .library.wisc.edu/FRUS/EFacs2/195557v12/reference/frus.frus195557v12.i0008.pdf.

NOTES FOR PAGE 20–22

49. "Telegram from the Embassy in the United Kingdom to the Department of State," (in editorial note 106), March 28, 1956, *FRUS 1955–1957*, vol. XV, pp. 421 ff; Dulles to Eisenhower, DDE Library. For Department of State, Central Files, 674.84A/3-2656, Top Secret, Eyes Only, http://images.library.wisc.edu/FRUS/EFacs2/195557v12 /reference/frus.frus195557v12.i0008.pdf. For a detailed account of U.S. maneuvers in the Middle East during this period, see the memoir of defense intelligence officer, CIA adviser, and military attaché Wilbur Crane Eveland, *Ropes of Sand*, p. 247. See also John Ranelagh, *The Agency: The Rise and Decline of the CIA, from Wild Bill Donovan to William Casey* (New York: Simon & Schuster, 1986), p. 298.

50. Malcolm H. Kerr, *The Arab Cold War: Gamal Abd Al-Nasir and His Rivals, 1958– 1970* (London: Oxford University Press, 1967); and Malcolm H. Kerr, *The Arab Cold War, 1958–1964: A Study of Ideology in Politics* (London: Oxford University Press, 1965).

51. Stephen E. Ambrose, *Eisenhower: Soldier and President* (New York: Simon Schuster, 1990), p. 360; and Rashid Khalidi, *Resurrecting Empire: Western Footprints and America's Perilous Path in the Middle East* (Boston: Beacon Press, 2004), p. 125.

52. Pan-Arabism is understood as the feeling of belonging to one Arab nation. Arab nationalism is understood as the particular nationalist movements that emerged in various Arab states. See Hans E. Tütsch, *Facets of Arab Nationalism* (Detroit: Wayne State University Press, 1965); Tawfik E. Farah, ed., *Pan-Arabism and Arab Nationalism: The Continuing Debate* (Boulder: Westview Press, 1987); and Bassam Tibi, *Arab Nationalism: A Critical Inquiry*, trans. Marion Farouk-Sluglett and Peter Sluglett (London: Macmillan Press, 1981). On the rise of pro-Nasserite parties, see Ellis Goldberg, "Gamal Abdel Nasser" in *Political Leaders of the Contemporary Middle East and North Africa: A Biographical Dictionary*, ed. Bernard Reich (New York: Greenwood Press, 1990), p. 384.

53. Saïd K. Aburish, *Nasser: The Last Arab* (New York: St. Martin's Press, 2004), p. 114; Helen Chapin Metz, ed., *Saudi Arabia: A Country Study* (Washington: Government Printing Office, 1992), http://countrystudies.us/saudi-arabia/, p. 249; Eveland, *Ropes of Sand*, p. 243; Yergin, *The Prize*, pp. 491–92; and Vassiliev, *The History of Saudi Arabia*, p. 351.

54. Dwight D. Eisenhower, "Special Message to the Congress on the Situation in the Middle East," January 5, 1957. Text of the document the President signed and transmitted to the Senate and the House of Representatives (H. Doc. 46, 85th Cong., 1st sess.), and the Address as reported from the floor appears in the *Congressional Record* (vol. 103, p. 181). For the text of this speech online, see Gerhard Peters and John T. Woolley, The American Presidency Project, Santa Barbara, CA, http://www .presidency.ucsb.edu/ws/?pid=11007.

55. By February, Jordan supported Saudi Arabia's alliance with Washington. Vassiliev, *The History of Saudi Arabia*, pp. 352–53.

56. Dwight D. Eisenhower, "Address at the Annual Luncheon of the Associated Press, New York City," April 25, 1955, Gerhard Peters and John T. Woolley, The American Presidency Project, http://www.presidency.ucsb.edu/ws/?pid=10459.

57. For an array of in-depth interviews with former American diplomats and senior American officials, see Robert Dreyfuss, *Devil's Game: How the United States Helped Unleash Fundamentalist Islam* (New York: Metropolitan Books, 2005), especially p. 125.

58. Johnson, *A Mosque in Munich*, pp. 41, 127–28.

59. Eveland, *Ropes of Sand*, pp. 244–45; for Eveland interview with author Kai Bird on July 25, 1982, see Bird, *Crossing Mandelbaum Gate*, pp. 195, 394.

60. Eveland, *Ropes of Sand*, p. 131.

61. Steven L. Spiegel, *The Other Arab-Israeli Conflict: Making America's Middle East Policy, from Truman to Reagan* (Chicago: University of Chicago Press, 1985), p. 88. Regarding anti-communist posters for Iraq, see United States Embassy, Iraq Cable from Edward S. Crocker II to the Department of State, "Anti-communist Poster Material Prepared by USIS Baghdad," March 10, 1951, National Archives. Record Group 59. Records of the Department of State. Decimal Files, 1950-1954, http://www.gwu.edu/~nsarchiv/NSAEBB/NSAEBB78/propaganda%20021.pdf. Regarding the offering of "leadership grants" to even "mildly pinkish" Iraqis, see United States Embassy, Iraq Cable from Edward S. Crocker II to the Department of State. "Foreign Leader Grants for Iraqis," March 26, 1951, National Archives. Record Group 59. Records of the Department of State. Decimal Files, 1950-1954, http://www.gwu.edu/~nsarchiv/NSAEBB/NSAEBB78/propaganda%20022.pdf; Dwight D. Eisenhower, "Statement by the President following the Landing of United States Marines at Beirut," July 15, 1958, Gerhard Peters and John T. Woolley, The American Presidency Project, http://www.presidency.ucsb.edu/ws/?pid=11133.

62. "Briefing notes by Director of Central Intelligence Dulles," July 14, 1958, *FRUS* 1958–1960, vol. XII, doc. 110, https://history.state.gov/historicaldocuments/frus1958-60v12/d110.

63. "Briefing Notes by Director of Central Intelligence Dulles," July 14, 1958, *FRUS* 1958–1960, vol. XII, Near East Region, doc. 110; "226. Memorandum of Discussion at the 373d Meeting of the National Security Council, Washington, July 24, 1958," Eisenhower Library, Whitman File, NSC Records. Top Secret; Eyes Only. Drafted by Boggs on July 25. The full text of the discussion of item 2 is scheduled for publication in volume XII, http://history.state.gov/historicaldocuments/frus1958-60v11/d226.

64. David Tal, "Seizing Opportunities: Israel and the 1958 Crisis in the Middle East," *Middle Eastern Studies* 37, no. 1 (January 2001): 143–58; David Allan Mayers, *George Kennan and the Dilemmas of U.S. Foreign Policy* (New York: Oxford University Press, 1988), p. 261. See also, "White House Memorandum of Conversation with the President," July 23, 1958, 3:00 p.m., pp. 1–3 (the Senate in the Sudan had unanimously condemned U.S.-UK action in the Near East); "226. Memorandum of Discussion at the 373d Meeting of the National Security Council, Washington, July 24, 1958," Eisenhower Library, Whitman File, NSC Records. Top Secret; Eyes Only. Drafted by Boggs on July 25. The full text of the discussion of item 2 is scheduled for publication in volume XII, http://history.state.gov/historicaldocuments/frus1958-60v11/d226. As Eisenhower acknowledged, there was still no answer to America's overall problem in the Middle East, that being Arab sympathies toward Nasser. See "26. Memorandum of Conference with President Eisenhower," Washington, July 20, 1958, 3:45 p.m. Eisenhower Library, Whitman File, Staff Memos, July 1958. Top Secret. Drafted by Goodpaster on July 21, http://www.history.state.gov/historicaldocuments/frus1958-60v12/d26#fn-source.

65. From an unpublished portion of Eisenhower's memoirs. Quoted in Ambrose, *Eisenhower*, p. 360.

66. "226. Memorandum of Discussion at the 373d Meeting of the National Security Council, Washington, July 24, 1958," Eisenhower Library, Whitman File, NSC Records. Top Secret; Eyes Only. Drafted by Boggs on July 25. The full text of the discussion of item 2 is scheduled for publication in volume XII, http://history.state.gov/historicaldocuments/frus1958-60v11/d226.

67. Kennedy to National Security staffer and Robert Komer in May 1961, as quoted in Michael O'Brien, *John F. Kennedy: A Biography* (New York: St. Martin's Press, 2005), p. 878.

68. "Special Message to the Congress on Urgent National Needs," May 25, 1961, Gerhard Peters and John T. Woolley, The American Presidency Project, http://www.presidency.ucsb.edu/ws/?pid=8151.

69. Safran, *Saudi Arabia*, p. 92; and Hart, *Saudi Arabia and the United States*, pp. 82–87.

70. For a definitive work on the Yemen crisis, see Warren Bass, *Support Any Friend: Kennedy's Middle East and the Making of the U.S.-Israel Alliance* (New York: Oxford University Press, 2003). Britain, Jordan, and Iran later backed the royalists, too. See "Yemen: Pax Americana?" *Time*, December 28, 1962; and "Yemen: Trouble for the Sons of Saud," *Time*, November 23, 1962.

71. Bass, *Support Any Friend*, p. 99.

72. Department of State, Central Files, 786H.11/9-2162. Secret. Cleared by Harold W. Glidden of INR, http://history.state.gov/historicaldocuments/frus1961-63v18/d51.

73. Department of State, Central Files, 611.86H/11–1262. Confidential. Drafted by Seelye. Kennedy Library, National Security Files, Countries Series, Yemen, 11/1/62–11/15/62, http://history.state.gov/historicaldocuments/frus1961-63v18/d96.

74. Dana Adams Schmidt, *Yemen: The Unknown War* (New York: Holt, Rinehart, and Winston, 1968), p. 189; Fawaz A. Gerges, "The Kennedy Administration and the Egyptian-Saudi Conflict in Yemen: Co-Opting Arab Nationalism," *Middle East Journal* 49, no. 2 (Spring 1995): 296; and Spiegel, *The Other Arab-Israeli Conflict*, p. 103.

75. Despite a UN-brokered disengagement agreement reached in the spring of 1963 and an Egyptian-Saudi ceasefire brokered in August 1965, both sides resumed hostilities. On Nasser's reassurances, see March 9, 1963, *New York Times* Chronology, John F. Kennedy Presidential Library and Museum, http://www.jfklibrary.org/Research/Research-Aids/Ready-Reference/New-York-Times-Chronology/Browse-by-Date/New-York-Times-Chronology-March-1963.aspx.

76. Talal bin Abdul Aziz Al Saud.

77. Faisal Bin Abd Al-Aziz Al Saud.

78. Safran, *Saudi Arabia*, p. 94; Simon Henderson, "After King Abdullah: Succession in Saudi Arabia," The Washington Institute for Near East Peace, Policy Focus no. 96 (August 2009); and Rayed Krimly, "Faisal Bin Abd Al-Aziz Al Saud," *Political Leaders of the Contemporary Middle East and North Africa: A Biographical Dictionary*, ed. Bernard Reich (New York: Greenwood Press, 1990), p. 182.

79. Robert Baer, *Sleeping with the Devil: How Washington Sold Our Soul for Saudi Crude* (New York: Crown Publishers, 2003), p. 99; and Bird, *Crossing Mandelbaum Gate*, p. 196.

80. Bird, *Crossing Mandelbaum Gate*, pp. 195–96; and Johnson, *A Mosque in Munich*, p. 238.

81. Gilles Kepel, *Jihad: The Trail of Political Islam* (Cambridge, MA: Harvard University Press, 2002), p. 52.

82. Dreyfuss, *Devil's Game*, p. 133; and Kepel, *Jihad*, p. 52.

83. Tellingly, the administration voiced regret that the issue was publicized, but never denied the story's validity. Bass, *Support Any Friend*, p. 130. The White House was considering another show of force in defense of the kingdom's southern border with Yemen after King Faisal fretted that Washington's fall 1962 fly-over covered only major Saudi cities, implying that border attacks were fair game.

84. "Saudi Arabia Lets Jews in US Units Serve on Her Soil," *New York Times*, June 10, 1963.

85. Bass, *Support Any Friend*, p. 131.

86. Hart, *Saudi Arabia and the United States*, pp. 210–33; and Safran, *Saudi Arabia*, pp. 96–97.

87. The deployment lasted until January 1964. "Editorial Note," *FRUS* 1961–1963, vol. XVIII, p. 581; Bass, *Support Any Friend*, pp. 129–30; Also see Spencer C. Tucker, ed., *The Encyclopedia of Middle East Wars: The United States in the Persian Gulf, Afghanistan, and Iraq Conflicts*, 5 vols. (Santa Barbara: ABC-CLIO, 2010), p. 523.

88. Douglas Little, *American Orientalism: The United States and the Middle East Since 1945* (Chapel Hill, NC: University of North Carolina Press, 2008), pp. 237, 239. Previous U.S. shows of force lacked a credible ability to defend the kingdom. See Tucker, *The Encyclopedia of Middle East Wars*, p. 523.

89. "Remarks at the Dinner of the Protestant Council of the City of New York," November 8, 1963, Gerhard Peters and John T. Woolley, The American Presidency Project, http://www.presidency.ucsb.edu/ws/?pid=9515.

90. "My Vietnam," quoted in Bird, *Crossing Mandelbaum Gate*, p. 193.

91. Former U.S. diplomat to Jeddah and Cairo Hermann Eilts said that Hassan al-Banna, the Brotherhood's founder, made frequent visits to Saudi Arabia "because Saudi Arabia was his principal source of financing." See Dreyfuss, *Devil's Game*, pp. 65, 126. See also Madawi Al-Rasheed, *A History of Saudi Arabia* (New York: Cambridge University Press, 2002), pp. 116, 144; Olivier Roy, *The Failure of Political Islam* (Cambridge, MA: Harvard University Press, 1998), p. 117; and Richard P. Mitchell, *The Society of the Muslim Brothers* (New York: Oxford University Press, 1993).

92. Some kings and princes were more pious than others, producing a struggle for supremacy between the royal family and the clerics. Dr. Ondrej Beranek, "The Sword and the Book: Implications of the Intertwining of the Saudi Ruling Family and the Religious Establishment," Crown Center for Middle East Studies, no. 28 (April 2008), http://www.brandeis.edu/crown/publications/meb/MEB28.pdf. Herman Eilts also describes the "constant tug of war" between the royal and religious families. See also Dreyfuss, *Devil's Game*, pp. 129–30. Salafism, like Wahhabism, is an umbrella term. The doctrine combines Sunni religious and cultural traditions from Egypt and other regions, and its revivalist movement, which seeks a return to Islam as practiced by Muhammad, began with this intermingling. For a comprehensive account of this history, see Abdullah M. Sindhi, "King Faisal and Pan-Islamism," in Willard L. Beling, ed., *King Faisal and the Modernisation of Saudi Arabia* (Boulder: Westview Press, 1980); al-Rasheed, *A History of Saudi Arabia*, pp. 122–23, 144; Trevor Stanley, "Understanding the Origins of Wahhabism and Salafism," *Terrorism Monitor* 3, no. 14 (July 15, 2005), http://www.jamestown.org/programs/tm/single/?tx_ttnews%5Btt _news%5D=528&tx_ttnews%5BbackPid%5D=180&no_cache=1#.VPYYZbPF-1I.; John L. Esposito, *Unholy War: Terror in the Name of Islam* (New York: Oxford University Press, 2003); David E. Long, *The Kingdom of Saudi Arabia* (Gainesville, FL: University of Florida Press, 1997); Eleanor Abdella Doumato, "Manning the Barricades: Islam according to Saudi Arabia's School Texts," *The Middle East Journal* 57, no. 2 (2003): 230–48; and Michaela Prokop, "Saudi Arabia: The Politics of Education," *International Affairs* 79, no. 1 (January 2003): 77–89.

93. Kepel, *Jihad*, p. 78; and Gold, *Hatred's Kingdom*, p. 92.

94. British journalist David Holden died mysteriously in Cairo while writing his book, *The House of Saud*. Richard Johns, *Financial Times* Middle East specialist, completed Holden's book. For more on Sheikh bin Baz, see David Holden and Richard Johns, *The House of Saud: The Rise and Rule of the Most Powerful Dynasty in the Arab World* (New York: Holt, Rinehart, and Winston, 1981), p. 262; and Gold, *Hatred's Kingdom*, p. 110.

95. Kepel, *Jihad*, p. 51.

96. Vassiliev, *The History of Saudi Arabia*, p. 435.

97. James Akins, U.S. Ambassador to Saudi Arabia, believed that Saudi universities should train "fewer mullahs." Saudis told Akins he was speaking beyond his competence. Akins thought it was rank stupidity. Other U.S. officials, though, raised few questions. Dreyfuss, *Devil's Game*, p. 129. On Adham's network of Islamist agents and the CIA encouraging Adham, see Bird, *Crossing Mandelbaum Gate*, pp. 139, 196.

98. Quoted in Bird, *Crossing Mandelbaum Gate*, p. 195.

99. Quoted in Dreyfuss, *Devil's Game*, p. 134.

100. Quoted in Gold, *Hatred's Kingdom*, p. 93.

101. "Remarks of Welcome to King Faisal of Saudi Arabia on the South Lawn at the White House," June 21, 1966, Gerhard Peters and John T. Woolley, The American Presidency Project, http://www.presidency.ucsb.edu/ws/?pid=27664.

102. Bass, *Support Any Friend*, p. 141. "Memorandum of Conversation," June 21, 1966, *FRUS* 1964–1968, vol. XXI, doc. 275. Johnson Library, National Security File, Country File, Saudi Arabia, Memos, vol. I, 12/63-4/67. Secret; Exdis. Drafted by Sabbagh on June 22, *FRUS* 1964–1968, vol. XXI, doc. 275, http://history.state.gov/historicaldocuments/frus1964-68v21/d275. The time of the meeting is from the President's Daily Diary. The memorandum is Part I of II; Part II is Document 276.

103. "Message by Ford, Rockefeller Flying to Convey Sympathy of American People," *New York Times*, March 26, 1975.

104. William B. Quandt, *Peace Process: American Diplomacy and the Arab-Israeli Conflict Since 1967* (Washington: Brookings Institution; Berkeley: University of California Press, 1993), p. 109.

105. Henry Kissinger, *White House Years* (Boston: Little, Brown, and Company, 1979), pp. 661, 656–66; Richard Valeriani, *Travels with Henry* (Boston: Houghton, Mifflin, 1979), p 310; Edward R. F. Sheehan, *The Israelis, the Arabs, and Kissinger* (New York: Reader's Digest Press, 1976), pp. 71, 234; Holden and Johns, *The House of Saud*, p. 271; and Richard Nixon, *RN: The Memoirs of Richard Nixon* (New York: Doubleday and Company, 1978), p. 1012.

106. Paul Lewis, "U.N. Repeals Its '75 Resolution Equating Zionism with Racism," *New York Times*, December 17, 1991; and Krimly, "Faisal Bin Abd Al-Aziz Al Saud."

107. Some factions threatened Jordan's ruling dynasty while others sought the destruction of Israel. National Archives and Records Administration, RG 59, Central Files 1964-66, POL7UAR. Limited Official Use. Drafted by Slator C. Blackiston Jr. (NEA/NE), *FRUS* 1964–1968, vol. XXI, doc. 1, http://history.state.gov/historical documents/frus1964-68v21/d1; P. J. Vatikiotis, *The History of Modern Egypt: From Muhammad Ali to Mubarak*, 3rd ed. (Baltimore: The Johns Hopkins University Press, 1985), pp. 405–06; Howard M. Sachar, *A History of Israel: From the Rise of Zionism to Our Time* (New York: Alfred A. Knopf, 1979), p. 616; and Robert McNamara, "Britain, Nasser, and the Outbreak of the Six Day War," *Journal of Contemporary History* 35, no. 4 (2000): 622.

108. Lyndon Johnson, *The Vantage Point: Perspectives of the Presidency 1963–1969* (New York: Holt, Rinehart, and Winston, 1971), p. 293.

109. Spiegel, *The Other Arab-Israeli Conflict*, pp. 119–20; "229. Memorandum for the Record," May 24, 1967. National Archives and Records Administration, RG 59, Records of the Department of State, Central Files, 1967-69, PET 6 SAUD. Secret; Exdis, *FRUS* 1964–1968, vol. XXXIV, doc. 229, http://history.state.gov/historicaldocuments/frus1964-68v34/d229. A note attached to the source text on White House letterhead reads, "May 24, 1967 To: S/S, Mr. Ben Read From: Bromley Smith FYI." A note on the source text by Harold Saunders reads, "President From—."

110. Michael B. Oren, *Six Days of War: June 1967 and the Making of the Modern Middle East* (New York: Oxford University Press, 2002), p. 84. Oren writes that Nasser's allegation concerned Israeli air cover. Joshua Pollack writes that Nasser's allegation was that U.S. and British carrier-based aircraft had attacked Egyptian airfields. Josh Pollack, "Saudi Arabia and the United States, 1931–2002," *Middle East Review of International Affairs* 6, no. 3 (September 2002): 81. In a letter to King Faisal, President Johnson wrote that the charges were "totally false." "Telegram from the Department of State to the Embassy in Saudi Arabia," June 8, 1967, *FRUS* 1964–1968, vol. XXI, Near East Region, Arabian Peninsula, doc. 290, http://history.state.gov/historicaldocuments/frus1964-68v21/d290. "Telegraph from the Department of State to the Embassy in Saudi Arabia, #290," June 8, 1967, *FRUS* 1964–1968, vol. XXI, doc. 290, National Archives and Records Administration, RG 59, Central Files 1967-69, POLSAUD-US. Secret; Immediate; Exdis. Drafted by Brewer on June 5, cleared by Battle and Bromley Smith, and approved by Secretary Rusk, http://history.state.gov/historicaldocuments/frus1964-68v21/d290#fn2.

111. Quoted in Thomas F. Brady, "Saudis Question Embargo on Oil," *New York Times*, July 1, 1967. Also see Yergin, *The Prize*, p. 555; and Brown, *Oil, God, and Gold*, pp. 268–80.

112. William B. Quandt, *Saudi Arabia in the 1980s: Foreign Policy, Security, and Oil* (Washington: The Brookings Institution, 1981), pp. 61–62.

113. The "three 'no's" has long been couched not as a preference of war over peace but as a firm rejection of coexistence with Israel. See Vatikiotis, *The History of Modern Egypt*, p. 408.

114. Kennedy was the first president to define U.S.-Israel relations as "special," but the defeat of the Soviet clients enhanced Israel's importance to Washington. Johnson noted the Russians "had lost their shirts" in the war. Robert Dallek, *Lyndon B. Johnson: Portrait of a President* (New York: Oxford University Press, 2005), p. 285. On U.S.-Israel relations, see Yitzhak Rabin, *The Rabin Memoirs* (Boston: Little, Brown, 1979), pp. 64–65; and Yaacov Bar-Siman-Tov, "The United States and Israel Since 1948: A 'Special Relationship'?" *Diplomatic History* 22, no. 2 (Spring 1998): 237–38. On states cutting diplomatic ties with the U.S., see Spiegel, *The Other Arab-Israeli Conflict*, p. 105, and George Lenczowski, *American Presidents and the Middle East* (Durham, NC: Duke University Press, 1990), pp. 112–13, 248. An April 1964 National Intelligence Estimate had warned presciently, "If US-Arab relations should deteriorate sharply, there would probably be a noticeable strengthening of Soviet influence." Similarly, the 1968 National Intelligence Estimate concluded, "The war and its aftermath have greatly reduced US influence in the Arab world and increased that of the USSR." Central Intelligence Agency, Job 79-R01012A, ODDI Registry of NIE and SNIE Files. Secret; Controlled Dissem., *FRUS* 1964–1968, vol. XXI, doc. 4, http://history.state.gov/historicaldocuments/frus1964-68v21/d4; and Central Intelligence Agency, Job 79-R01012A, ODDI Registry of NIE and SNIE Files. Secret; Controlled Dissem., *FRUS* 1964–1968, vol. XXI, doc. 32, http://history.state.gov/historicaldocuments/frus1964-68v21/d32.

115. See "297. Telegram From the Embassy in Saudi Arabia to the Department of State /1/Jidda, June 23, 1967, 1528Z. Source: National Archives and Records Administration, RG 59, Central Files 1967-69, POL 27 ARAB-ISR. Secret; Priority; Limdis. Repeated to USUN, http://www.state.gov/www/about_state/history/vol_xxi/zb.html.

116. See Moshe Dayan, *Breakthrough: A Personal Account of the Egypt-Israel Peace Negotiations* (New York: Random House, 1981), p. 87; Eitan Habar, Zeev Schiff, and

Ehud Yaari, *The Year of the Dove* (New York: Bantam, 1979), pp. 13–14; and John Norton Moore, ed., *The Arab-Israeli Conflict: Readings and Documents*, vol. 4 (Princeton: Princeton University Press, 1974), pp. 1106–25.

117. On Saudi concerns, see Yergin, *The Prize*, p. 595.

118. James E. Akins, "The Oil Crisis: This Time the Wolf Is Here," *Foreign Affairs* 51, no. 3 (April 1973): 462–90.

119. Jim Hoagland, "Faisal Warns US on Israel," *Washington Post*, July 6, 1973; Jim Hoagland, "Saudis Ponder Whether to Produce the Oil US Needs," *Washington Post*, July 11, 1973; and Yergin, *The Prize*, pp. 596–97.

120. Yergin, *The Prize*, p. 597. Also see Chaim Herzog, *The Arab Israeli Wars: War and Peace in the Middle East, from the War of Independence through Lebanon* (New York: Vintage Books, 1983), p. 302; and Safran, *Saudi Arabia*, pp. 152–55.

121. James Schlesinger, *The House of Saud*, directed by Jihan El-Tahri (Paris: Alegria Productions, 2004), DVD.

122. Henry Kissinger, *Diplomacy* (New York: Simon & Schuster, 1995), p. 739; Yergin, *The Prize*, pp. 602–03; Spiegel, *The Other Arab-Israeli Conflict*, p. 247; and Nixon, *RN: The Memoirs of Richard Nixon*, p. 924.

123. Spiegel, *The Other Arab-Israeli Conflict*, p. 243; and Yergin, *The Prize*, p. 604.

124. Bird, *Crossing Mandelbaum Gate*, p. 222.

125. For Kissinger's perspective, see Henry Kissinger, *Years of Upheaval* (Boston: Little, Brown, 1982), pp. 468–515. Nixon's take can be found in Nixon, *RN: The Memoirs of Richard Nixon*, p. 787.

126. William B. Quandt, *Decade of Decisions: American Policy toward the Arab-Israeli Conflict, 1967–1976* (Berkeley: University of California Press, 1977), p. 184; Moshe Dayan, *Moshe Dayan: Story of My Life* (New York: Da Capo Press, 1992), pp. 421–22; and Nixon, *RN: The Memoirs of Richard Nixon*, pp. 927–28. The airlift proceeded on the condition that Israeli cargo plane would have the El Al markings painted out, as not to endanger U.S. interests by assisting an ally "too visibly." The planes, however, were detected. Memcon between Dinitz and Kissinger, 9 October 1973, 6:10–6:35 p.m. Source: RG 59, SN 70-73, Pol Isr-US, http://www.gwu.edu/~nsarchiv/NSAEBB/NSAEBB98/octwar-21b.pdf; William Quandt to Kissinger, "Middle Eastern Issues," October 9, 1973, Source: NPMP, NSCF, box 664, Middle East War Memos & Misc. Oct. 6–Oct. 17, 1973, http://www.gwu.edu/~nsarchiv/NSAEBB/NSAEBB98/octwar-22.pdf. Also see Yergin, *The Prize*, pp. 598–617; and Safran, *Saudi Arabia*, pp. 556–60.

127. Aramco president Frank Jungers claimed that the Saudis insisted on specific instructions to ensure embargo, setting up a system to determine "where the oil actually ended up, every barrel," under threat of complete nationalization. Aramco also got Saudi Arabia's tacit permission to supply oil to America's Sixth and Seventh Fleets. But it's alleged that Aramco ignored this. Brown, *Oil, God, and Gold*, pp. 294–96.

128. Kamal Adham was the conduit for President Sadat and Secretary Kissinger in the early 1970s. Sadat's wife also had business ventures with Kamal Adham. Holden and Johns, *The House of Saud*, pp. 289–93; Kissinger, *White House Years*, p. 1293.

129. The U.S. bill on foreign oil climbed from $3.9 billion to $24 billion between 1972 and 1973, and inflation doubled in many Western European nations. Still, in 1973, only 10 percent of U.S. total oil consumption came from the Persian Gulf and North Africa. See Yergin, *The Prize*, pp. 590–94; and "King Faisal: Man of the Year," *Time*, January 6, 1975.

130. "Excerpts from the Kissinger News Conference," *New York Times*, November 22, 1973. Kissinger implied the embargo was an "actual strangulation of the industrialized world." "Kissinger on Oil, Food, and Trade," *Business Week*, January 13, 1975, p. 69. President Ford also referred to the embargo as "economic strangulation." See "Gerald Ford: They Will See Something Is Being Done," *Time*, January 20, 1975, p. 21. Defense Secretary Schlesinger indicated "conceivably military measures in response" in the event of another oil embargo. "Now a Tougher U.S.: Interview with James R. Schlesinger, Secretary of Defense," *U.S. News & World Report*, May 26, 1975, pp. 26–27. Articles and essays on this confrontational approach include Robert Tucker, "Oil: The Issue of American Intervention," *Commentary*, January 1975; Tucker (writing under a pseudonym), "Seizing Arab Oil," *Harper's*, March 1975; Glen Frankel, "U.S. Mulled Seizing Oil Fields in 1973," *Washington Post*, January 1, 2004; and Owen Bowcott, "UK Feared Americans Would Invade Gulf During 1973 Oil Crisis," *The Guardian* (London), January 1, 2004.

131. Stephen Hayes, "Joint Economic Commissions as Instruments of US Foreign Policy in the Middle East," *Middle East Journal* 31, no. 1 (Winter 1977): 16–30. Edward R. F. Sheehan, *The Arabs, Israelis, and Kissinger: A Secret History of American Diplomacy in the Middle East* (New York: Reader's Digest Press, 1976), p. 116; Quandt, *Decade of Decisions*, p. 232; Kissinger, *Years of Upheaval*, p. 975; Henry Kissinger, *Years of Renewal* (New York: Simon & Schuster, 1999), p. 677.

132. "Remarks at the Conclusion of Discussions with King Faisal of Saudi Arabia," June 15, 1974, Gerhard Peters and John T. Woolley, The American Presidency Project, http://www.presidency.ucsb.edu/ws/?pid=4254.

133. Thomas W. Lippman, *Saudi Arabia on the Edge: The Uncertain Future of an American Ally* (Washington: Potomac Books, 2012); Anthony Sampson, *The Arms Bazaar: From Lebanon to Lockheed* (New York: Viking Press, 1977), pp. 331–37; and Martin Tolchin, "Foreigners' Political Roles in US Grow by Investing," *New York Times*, December 30, 1985. By 1979, American companies signed nearly $6 billion in nonmilitary contracts in Saudi Arabia. Tom McHale, "Flow of Funds," in *Saudi Arabia: A MEED Special Report* (Dubai: MEED, 1980), pp. 94–95.

134. Saudi Arabia, Kuwait, and the United Arab Emirates set up a special fund through which Syria and Egypt each received $570 million, Jordan $300 million, and the PLO $28 million. Esposito, *Unholy War*, pp. 107–8. These Western financial institutions acquired ownership, maintained complete Islamic subsidiaries, and opened branches as the Saudis invested their capital. In the late 1990s, Citibank's largest individual shareholder was the Saudi prince Al Walid Bin Talal. See Ibrahim Warde, *Islamic Finance in the Global Economy* (Edinburgh: Edinburgh University Press, 2000). Also see Clement M. Henry, "Islamic Financial Movements: Midwives of Political Change in the Middle East?" paper prepared for the 2001 Annual Meetings of the American Political Science Association, San Francisco (August 30–September 6, 2001), http://www.ifisa.co.za/Articles/Islamic%20Banking/Islamic%20Movements%20in%20finance_Banking.pdf; and Josh Martin, "Citibank Goes Islamic," *The Middle East* (London), July 1, 1996.

135. Khlaid bin Abdul-Aziz Al Saud.

136. Fahd bin Abd al-Aziz.

137. Vassiliev, *The History of Saudi Arabia*, p. 395.

138. Bernard Gwertzman, "US Jets Will Visit Saudi Arabia as Show of Support in Tense Area," *New York Times*, January 11, 1979. Saudi ambassador to the United States Prince Bandar said that the consequences were devastating and lived on. "We don't

want you to put out a hand and then pull it back," the ambassador said. Quoted in Bob Woodward, *The Commanders* (New York: Simon & Schuster, 1991), p. 240.

139. Quoted in Peter A. Iseman, "Iran's War of Words against Saudi Arabia," *The Nation*, April 19, 1980. Also see James Buchan, "Secular and Religious Opposition in Saudi Arabia," in *State, Society, and Economy in Saudi Arabia*, pp. 117–20.

140. Quoted in Buchan, "Secular and Religious Opposition in Saudi Arabia," p. 122; Also see Yaroslav Trofimov, *The Siege of Mecca: The Forgotten Uprising in Islam's Holiest Shrine* (New York: Doubleday, 2007); and Steve Coll, *Ghost Wars: The Secret History of the CIA, Afghanistan, and bin Laden, from the Soviet Invasion to September 10, 2001* (New York: Penguin Books, 2004), pp. 27–29.

141. Robin Wright, *Sacred Rage: The Wrath of Militant Islam* (New York: Touchstone Press, 1985), p. 148; and Daniel Benjamin and Steven Simon, *The Age of Sacred Terror* (New York: Random House, 2002), p. 90.

142. Quoted in Bird, *Crossing Mandelbaum Gate*, p. 154.

143. Wright, *The Looming Tower*, p. 147; and Carmen Bin Laden, *Inside the Kingdom*.

144. Dreyfuss, *Devil's Game*, p. 258.

145. U.S. Embassy in Kabul to Department of State, Airgram A-77, "Afghanistan Clerical Unrest: A Tentative Assessment," June 24, 1970, Confidential, 7 pp. Source: National Archives, Record Group 59, Subject-Numeric Files, 1970 (hereinafter SN 70 -73), Pol 23-8 AFG, http://www.gwu.edu/~nsarchiv/NSAEBB/NSAEBB59/zahir02.pdf.

146. An October State Department cable reported: "The Saudis interpret Moscow's take over in Afghanistan last year as part of a Soviet-directed campaign to encircle the Persian Gulf and the Arabian Peninsula with radical regimes in preparation for the subversion of the conservative oil-rich monarchies." Marin J. Strmecki, "Power Assessment: Measuring Soviet Power in Afghanistan" (PhD diss., Georgetown University, 1994); and Bronson, *Thicker than Oil*, pp. 154–60n.

147. Zbigniew Brzezinski, *Power and Principle: Memoirs of the National Security Advisor, 1977–1981* (New York: Farrar Straus and Giroux, 1983), p. 449.

148. "The State of the Union Address Delivered before a Joint Session of the Congress," January 23, 1980, Gerhard Peters and John T. Woolley, The American Presidency Project, http://www.presidency.ucsb.edu/ws/?pid=33079.

149. "The President's News Conference," October 1, 1981, Gerhard Peters and John T. Woolley, The American Presidency Project, http://www.presidency.ucsb.edu/ws/?pid=44327.

150. David E. Long, "Fahd Bin Abd Al-Aziz Al-Saud," in *Political Leaders of the Contemporary Middle East and North Africa*, p. 178.

151. Esposito, *Unholy War*, p. 86; and Reinhard Schulze, *A Modern History of the Islamic World*, trans. Azizeh Azodi (New York: New York University Press, 2002), p. 201.

152. The Saudis also created the Riyadh-based GCC with conservative, Sunni-ruled regimes in the United Arab Emerates, Bahrain, Oman, Qatar, and Kuwait to regulate finance, trade, customs, and tourism; foster scientific and technical progress; and establish a unified military presence. See Safran, *Saudi Arabia*, pp. 172–76.

153. "Transcript of President's News Conference on Foreign and Domestic Politics," *New York Times*, October 2, 1981; Esposito, *Unholy War*, p. 86. On Reagan's anger at Israeli influence, see Alexander M. Haig Jr., *Caveat: Realism, Reagan, and Foreign Policy* (New York: Macmillan, 1984), pp. 189–90.

154. Majid Khadduri, *The Gulf War: The Origins and Implications of the Iran-Iraq Conflict* (New York: Oxford University Press, 1988), p. 124. Reagan threatened to punish one

senator by closing a base in his district. See Melinda Beck, "AWACS: The Final Days," *Newsweek*, November 2, 1981. Also see Robin Allen, "Saudi Arabia Builds Defence of the Realm," *Financial Times* (London), November 23, 1988; Jim Mann, "Threat to Mideast Military Balance; U.S. Caught Napping by Sino-Saudi Missile Deal," *Los Angeles Times*, May 4, 1988; and John M. Goshko and Don Oberdorfer, "Chinese Sell Saudis Missiles Capable of Covering Mideast," *Washington Post*, March 18, 1988.

155. Turki bin Faisal al-Saud.

156. Saudi General Khaled bin Sultan relates that King Fahd sensed it would be unwise "to tie ourselves to an alliance which was likely to arouse the hostility of the Arab and Muslim world." HRH General Khaled bin Sultan with Patrick Seale, *Desert Warrior: A Personal View of the Gulf War by the Joint Forces Commander* (New York: HarperCollins, 1995), p. 25; Hart, *Saudi Arabia and the United States*, p. 85–89; and Trofimov, *The Siege of Mecca*, p. 172.

157. In the mid 1980s, the president secretly shipped 400 Stinger missiles to Saudi Arabia for short-range air defense. Michael H. Armacost, "US Response to Saudi Request for Military Assistance-Transcript," US Department of State Bulletin, July 1984; Bernard Gwertzman, "Senators Assail Arms Sale to Saudis," *New York Times*, June 6, 1984; Robert M. Gates, *From the Shadows: The Ultimate Insider's Story of Five Presidents and How They Won the Cold War* (New York: Simon & Schuster, 1997), p. 311; Jeff Gerth, "The White House Crisis; Evidence Points to Big Saudi Role in Iranian and Contra Arms Deals," *New York Times*, November 30, 1986; David B. Ottaway, "Saudi Envoy Has Credibility Woes," *Washington Post*, February 28, 1987; and Lawrence E. Walsh, *Firewall: The Iran-Contra Conspiracy and Cover-Up* (New York: W.W. Norton, 1998), pp. 389–92.

158. Coll, *Ghost Wars*, p. 81; and Steven V. Roberts, "Prop for U.S. Policy: Secret Saudi Funds," *New York Times*, June 21, 1987. For more on aid policies, see Thomas W. Lippman, "Saudis Pledge $1 Billion Aid to Africa; Saudis Pledge $1 Billion Aid at Afro-Arab Talks in Cairo," *Washington Post*, March 8, 1977. Also see Bronson, *Thicker than Oil*, p. 135; and Kenneth Labich, "Saudi Power," *Newsweek* (International Edition), March 6, 1978.

159. Passed the House by a bipartisan vote of 411–0. See Gates, *From the Shadows*, p. 298.

160. For the $32 million figure, and the entire argument more generally, see Jonathan Marshall, "Saudi Arabia and the Reagan Doctrine," *Middle East Report* 18 (November/December 1988), http://www.merip.org/mer/mer155/saudi-arabia-reagan-doctrine. (Marshall also cites *San Francisco Examiner*, March 12, 1987; and *Insight*, July 6, 1987.) See House of Representatives, Select Committee to Investigate Covert Arms Transactions with Iran, and Senate Select Committee on Secret Military Assistance to Iran and the Nicaraguan Opposition, report, "Iran-Contra Affair" (Washington: GPO, 1987), pp. 5, 45, 119–20, 128, https://archive.org/details/reportofcongress87unit. Related to the above citation (US Gov), Saudi Arabia is "Country 2": see "The Iran-Contra Report," The American Presidency Project, http://www.presidency.ucsb.edu/PS157/assignment%20files%20public/congressional%20report%20key%20sections.htm. Bob Woodward, *Veil: The Secret Wars of the CIA, 1981–1987* (New York: Simon & Schuster, 1987), p. 401.

161. Sen. John Glenn (D-OH), testimony before the Senate Committee on Foreign Relations, U.S.—Pakistan Nuclear Issues, July 30, 1992, http:// www.fas.org/news /pakistan/1992/920731.htm. On dollar for dollar, see Gates, *From the Shadows*, p. 148. Also see Michael Scheuer, *Through Our Enemies Eyes: Osama bin Laden, Radical Islam*

and the Future of America (Herndon, VA: Potomac Books, 2003), p. 41; Peter Dale Scott, *The Road to 9/11: Wealth, Empire, and the Future of America* (Berkeley, CA: University of California Press, 2007), pp. 62–63; and Jonathan Beaty and S. C. Gwynne, *The Outlaw Bank: A Wild Rise Into the Secret Heart of BCCI* (New York: Random House, 1993).

162. Coll, *Ghost Wars*, pp. 128–35; Adam Curtis, *The Power of Nightmares: The Rise of the Politics of Fear* (London: British Broadcasting Corporation, 2004), TV miniseries; James Bryce, "Arab Veterans of the Afghan War," *Jane's Intelligence Review* 7, no. 4 (1995); and Peter L. Bergen, *Holy War, Inc.: Inside the Secret World of Osama Bin Laden* (New York: Free Press, 2001), p. 70.

163. Chris Hedges, "Muslim Militants Have Afghan Links," *New York Times*, March 28, 1993, http://www.nytimes.com/1993/03/28/world/muslim-militants-share -afghan-link.html?pagewanted=all&src=pm; Esposito, *Unholy War*, pp. 87–88; Gold, *Hatred's Kingdom*, p. 94; and Kepel, *Jihad*, p. 147.

164. Coll, *Ghost Wars*, pp. 83, 154.

165. Gold, *Hatred's Kingdom*, p. 121.

166. Coll, *Ghost Wars*, pp. 278–79, 512.

167. Joe Stephens and David B. Ottoway, "From U.S., the ABC's of Jihad: Violent Soviet-Era Textbooks Complicate Afghan Education Efforts," *Washington Post*, March 2, 2002.

168. Thomas L. Friedman, "Foreign Affairs: In Pakistan, It's Jihad 101," *New York Times*, November 3, 2001.

Chapter 2

1. Alan Greenspan, *The Age of Turbulence: Adventures in a New World* (New York: Penguin, 2007), p. 463.

2. PBS *Frontline*, "Saudi Time Bomb? Interview James Baker," October 1, 2001.

3. "Deputy Secretary Wolfowitz Interview with Sam Tannenhaus, *Vanity Fair*," Defense.gov, May 9, 2003, http://www.defense.gov/transcripts/transcript.aspx ?transcriptid=2594. According to CNN's Peter Bergen, who recounts his meeting with bin Laden, what most enraged the Saudi terrorist was the American military presence in Saudi Arabia. Incensed that the Saudis invited U.S. troops to their defense after the Iraqi invasion of Kuwait, bin Laden—like many Muslims—considered the continued presence of these armed infidels in Saudi Arabia the greatest possible desecration of the holy land and contended that they must be driven out.

4. Bureau for International Narcotics and Law Enforcement Affairs, *International Narcotics Control Strategy Report—Volume II: Money Laundering and Financial Crimes* (Washington: Department of State, 2006), http://2001-2009.state.gov/p/nea/ci /sa/80179.htm.

5. Azzam studied and taught Islamic politics in Egypt and Jordan, but when his views became too subversive he found refuge in the kingdom, where he won appointment to the faculty of King Abdulaziz University. By 1981 he was sent to Islamic University in Islamabad, Pakistan, with $35 million in Saudi funds. See Steve Coll, *The Bin Ladens: An Arabian Family in the American Century* (New York: Penguin Press, 2008), p. 253.

6. The Afghan war was meant to strengthen the *umma* to liberate Palestine. The larger war with Israel, the West, and other unbelievers was part of some millenarian conflict leading to Judgment Day, as forecast in the Quran. See Coll, *The Bin Ladens*, pp. 256–57.

7. Bin Laden leveraged his experience with advertisers and promotional products from his earlier years at his family's Bin Laden Company. See Coll, *The Bin Ladens*, p. 259.

8. Pakistan officially restricted U.S. and Saudi access to rebels. But for narrative accounts of bin Laden's connections to GID, see James Risen, *State of War: The Secret History of the CIA and the Bush Administration* (New York: Simon and Schuster, 2006), p. 180; Lawrence Wright, *The Looming Tower: Al-Qaeda and the Road to 9/11* (New York: Knopf, 2006), p. 103–20; and Steve Coll, *Ghost Wars: The Secret History of the CIA, Afghanistan, and bin Laden, from the Soviet Invasion to September 10, 2001* (New York: Penguin Press, 2004), pp. 87–88.

9. After Turki Al-Faisal, as chief of foreign intelligence, named Ahmed Badeeb his chief of staff. For Badeeb quote about bin Laden, see Coll, *The Bin Ladens*, p. 295.

10. Coll, *The Bin Ladens*, p. 251.

11. According to Pulitzer Prize-winning journalist and author Steve Coll—who wrote that as early as 1988, wealthy Saudi merchants may have been among the most generous contributors to bin Laden's fundraising network and militia—American investigators and prosecutors confirmed that the documents uncovered were authentic and credible. See Coll, *The Bin Ladens*, p. 341–42. For more on bin Laden and Saudi charities, see "Government's Evidentiary Proffer Supporting the Admissibility of Co-Conspirator Statements," *United States v. Enaam Arnaout*, No. 02-CR-892 (N.D. Ill, filed January 6, 2003). For more on the trove of al Qaeda documents, see Glenn R. Simpson, "List of Early al Qaeda Donors Points to Saudi Elite, Charities," *Wall Street Journal*, March 18, 2003.

12. National Commission on Terrorist Attacks upon the United States, *The 9/11 Commission Report: Final Report of the National Commission on Terrorist Attacks upon the United States* (hereafter *The 9/11 Report*), (Washington: National Commission on Terrorist Attacks upon the United States, 2004), pp. 372.

13. Robert M. Guido, "U.S. Efforts to Combat Terrorism Financing: Progress Made and Future Challenges," *Small Wars Journal*, August 19, 2010.

14. Coll, *The Bin Ladens*, p. 341. *Al-Jihad*, a magazine supported by the Services Office, praised Saudi support of seven charities in its December 1986 issue. One was the Mecca-based Muslim World League. See Alex Strick van Linschoten and Felix Kuehn, *An Enemy We Created: The Myth of the Taliban–Al Qaeda Merger* (New York: Oxford University Press, 2012), pp. 359–60, n140.

15. The militarily defenseless Kuwaitis, despite their purchase of sophisticated American weaponry, used their commanding economic positions to pay 55 percent of what would become Operation Desert Storm. Saudi Arabia and Kuwait paid approximately $33 billion toward the total cost of Desert Storm and Desert Shield, which was $60 billion. The U.S. share was only $6 billion (10 percent), according to a Defense Department press release (125-M) issued on May 5, 1992. Oil revenues are 70–80 percent of Saudi government revenues. See the citation in Jerry Taylor and Peter VanDoren, "The Soft Case for Soft Energy," *Journal of International Affairs* 53, no. 1 (1999): 225.

16. Bin Laden claimed he worked for the true interest of the royal family. At the time, Saudi Bin Laden Group, when Osama bin Laden was still a shareholder, signed contracts with the U.S. Army to build facilities supporting U.S. troop presence. Bin Laden likely profited from those construction projects. Coll, *The Bin Ladens*, pp. 375–76.

17. *Ulema* (sometimes spelled *ulama*) were trained in the interpretation of Islamic (*Sharia*) law, Islamic jurisprudence, and Islamic sciences and doctrines.

18. Statement of Secretary of Defense Dick Cheney, "Crisis in the Persian Gulf Region: U.S. Policy Options and Implications: Hearings before the U.S. Senate Armed Services Committee," 101st Congress, 2nd Session (1990).

19. The oil myth is based on the false assumption of a "fair and reasonable price" for oil. The reality is that oil is a commodity openly traded on the worldwide market, and the price of oil is determined by supply and demand, not by some perception of what it should cost. As Massachusetts Institute of Technology economist Morris Adelman points out, "The world oil market, like the world ocean, is one great pool. The price is the same at every border. Who exports the oil Americans consume is irrelevant." For more on the myth of oil security, see Morris Adelman, *Genie out of the Bottle: World Oil since 1970* (Cambridge, MA: MIT Press, 2008); and Jerry Taylor and Peter Van Doren, "The Energy Security Question," *Georgetown Journal of Law and Public Policy* 6, no. 2 (Summer 2008): 475–85.

20. The only real issue was immediate price spikes: the 1970s oil shocks. Only after coalition forces entered the conflict did Saddam's forces set fire to hundreds of Kuwaiti oil wells. Even then, that action failed to generate a major imbalance in the world's oil market.

21. George Bush, *All the Best, George Bush: My Life in Letters and Other Writings* (New York: Scribner, 1990), p. 476. The majority of foreign securities are U.S. treasury bills, of which Saudi Arabia has considerable holdings, and private Saudi business families hold large portfolio investments in the U.S. See U.S. Department of the Treasury, "Major Foreign Holders of Treasury Securities," http://www.treasury.gov/resource -center/data-chart-center/tic/Documents/mfh.txt.

22. For more on U.S. aid to Saddam during the Iran-Iraq War (1980–1988), see Shane Harris and Matthew M. Aid, "Exclusive: CIA Files Prove America Helped Saddam as He Gassed Iran," *ForeignPolicy.com*, August 26, 2013.

23. The *New York Times* reported that General H. Norman Schwarzkopf, the commander of U.S. military forces during the Persian Gulf War, reduced Iraq's "combat effectiveness" by 50 to 100 percent. See Eric Schmitt, "Study Lists Lower Tally of Iraqi Troops in Gulf War," *New York Times*, April 24, 1992. On discrepancies over the threat posed by Saddam, see Scott Peterson, "In War, Some Facts Less Factual," *Christian Science Monitor*, September 6, 2002; and Dave Kehr, "The Hidden Wars of Desert Storm: Questioning U.S. Motives in the Persian Gulf War," *New York Times*, April 20, 2001.

24. Ann Reilly Dowd and Suneel Ratan, "How Bush Decided," *Fortune*, February 11, 1991.

25. Kuwait, Iraq's "small and helpless neighbor," was not attacked, but "crushed," and the Kuwaiti people "brutalized." For more, see George Bush, "Address to the Nation Announcing Allied Military Action in the Persian Gulf," January 16, 1991," Gerhard Peters and John T. Woolley, The American Presidency Project, http://www .presidency.ucsb.edu/ws/?pid=19222.

26. Implying such control was political, not purely economic. Secretary Baker later said about U.S. involvement in the Middle East, "We're their security because we have a self-interest in making sure that those energy reserves in the Persian Gulf *don't fall under the control of a country that is adverse to the United States.*" [Emphasis added.] PBS *Frontline*, "Saudi Time Bomb?"

27. George Bush, "Address before a Joint Session of the Congress on the Cessation of the Persian Gulf Conflict," March 6, 1991," Gerhard Peters and John T. Woolley, The American Presidency Project, http://www.presidency.ucsb.edu/ws/?pid=19364.

28. In November, 47 women shocked Saudi society by driving through Riyadh in violation of the kingdom's ban on female drivers. In early 1991, 43 liberal-leaning businessmen, journalists, and university professors signed a petition to Fahd asking for broader political participation. Coll, *The Bin Ladens*, p. 378.

29. Khashoggi, bin Laden, and others feared more than individual irreligious or sinful behavior, such as "a mass movement of secularization, mixed schools, top-down changes." See Coll, *The Bin Ladens*, pp. 260, 378–79.

30. Osama bin Laden, *Messages to the World: The Statements of Osama bin Laden*, ed. Bruce Lawrence (London, UK: Verso, 2005), p. 203.

31. In Yemen, before his retreat from Afghanistan, bin Laden was sponsoring militants attempting to overthrow South Yemen's communist government. Later that decade, bin Laden's militants received advice and training from Shiite Muslim terrorists, although their intra-Islamic enmity could take collaboration only so far. For more, see *The 9/11 Commission Report*, p. 240.

32. About private charitable funds intended for poor refugees rather than terrorists, a Benevolence International Foundation official stated, "That is our mission—Lying to people." Also, BIF began services in Sudan "after the agreement of *the base* in Sudan with the Sudanese Government." [Emphasis in original.] For more on the training of Sudanese forces, see *United States v. Enaam Arnaout*, p. 22. For more on BIF activities, see pp. 48, 58. The Benevolence International Foundation, according to its own report, supported jihad, mujahideen, and, in the service of Islamic proselytizing (*dawah*), "to make Islam supreme on this Earth." The Benevolence International Foundation was formerly known as Lajnatt Al-Birr Al-Islamiah. See *United States v. Enaam Arnaout*, pp. 51, 57.

33. An article from the era reported that the Black Swans spent around $700,000 per month in cash on weapons, equipment, and supplies. The article, citing Brigadier Tiric, states, "He said that some of the funds come through the army's general command but that most come from 'private sources.'" See Chuck Sudetic, "Bosnia's Elite Force: Fed, Fit, Muslim," *New York Times*, June 16, 1995. See also *United States v. Enaam Arnaout*, pp. 25, 66, 68. In addition, Pulitzer Prize–winning reporter Karen Elliot House, who spent the past 30 years writing about Saudi Arabia as a diplomatic correspondent, foreign editor, and publisher of the *Wall Street Journal*, writes that the Saudi government "gave billions of dollars to aid jihadists fighting in Afghanistan, Chechnya, and Bosnia." See Karen Elliot House, *On Saudi Arabia: Its People, Past, Religion, Fault Lines—and Future* (New York: Knopf, 2012), p. 29.

34. Office of Public Affairs, "Treasury Designates Benevolence International Foundation and Related Entities as Financiers of Terrorism," November 19, 2002, http://www.investigativeproject.org/documents/misc/27.pdf.

35. For more on bin Laden's desire to extend his operations outside of Afghanistan before the end of the Afghan-Soviet War, see Michael Scheuer, *Osama bin Laden* (New York: Oxford University Press, 2012), p. 104. On training camps in Sudan, see PBS *Frontline*, "Osama bin Laden: A Chronology of His Political Life," http://www.pbs.org/wgbh/pages/frontline/shows/binladen/etc/cron.html; and Jeff Gerth and Judith Miller, "Funds for Terrorists Traced to Persian Gulf Businessmen," *New York Times*, August 14, 1996.

36. For more on the training facility in Riyadh, see "U.S. Vows Terrorist Bomb 'Won't Affect Saudi Relationship,'" *CNN*, November 13, 1995.

37. Thomas W. Simons Jr., "Pakistan, Islamic Terror and Hua (96ISLAMABAD5972)," American Embassy Islamabad, July 14, 1996.

38. And by 1997, Al Haramain Islamic Foundation (HIF) employees in Kenya were arrested for planning a terrorist attack against the U.S., with some planning conducted inside the HIF office. See *The 9/11 Commission Report*, chap. 7, "Al Haramain Case Study." A U.S. State Department memorandum later uncovered that top-level HIF

officials condoned funding militants, and that charity field offices and representatives around the world, including HIF headquarters in Riyadh, appeared to provide financial and logistical support to al Qaeda. Colin Powell, "Terrorist Financing–Updated Nonpaper on Al Haramain (03STATE23994)," Washington, D.C., January 28, 2003.

39. Douglas Jehl, "Saudis Are Shutting Down a Charity Tied to Terrorists," *New York Times*, June 3, 2004; *The 9/11 Commission Report*, chap. 7, "Al Haramain Case Study."

40. "U.S. Strength in the Persian Gulf," *Washington Post*, February 24, 1998, http://www.washingtonpost.com/wp-srv/inatl/longterm/iraq/military/usstrength.htm.

41. His fatwa appeared in an edition of the London-based, Arabic-language newspaper *Al-Quds Al-Arabi*. See "Bin Laden's Fatwa," PBS *NewsHour*, August 23, 1996, http://www.pbs.org/newshour/updates/military/july-dec96/fatwa_1996.html. According to bin Laden biographer Yossef Bodansky, radical clerics offered Quranic backing to bin Laden's bloodshed, insisting that all methods of war, including terrorism, are justified in the battle against the infidels. See Yossef Bodansky, *Bin Laden: The Man Who Declared War on America* (New York: Random House, 2001).

42. Michael Scheuer, "Extraordinary Rendition in U.S. Counterterrorism Policy: The Impact on Transatlantic Relations," Joint Hearing before the Subcommittee on International Organizations, Human Rights, and Oversight, and the Subcommittee on Europe, April 17, 2007, p. 32.

43. "CNN March 1997 Interview with Osama bin Laden," news.findlaw.com/cnn/docs/binladen/binladenintvw-cnn.pdf.

44. "Bin Laden's Fatwa," PBS *NewsHour*.

45. See the Quran, Surahs 5:32 and 5:33, for another opinion. "CNN March 1997 Interview with Osama bin Laden" For more on the deaths of Iraqi children, see UNICEF, "Iraq Surveys Show 'Humanitarian Emergency,'" Unicef.org, August 12, 1999, http://www.unicef.org/newsline/99pr29.htm.

46. The front, including three other militant groups, said in its founding manifesto: "We—with God's help—call on every Muslim . . . to comply with God's order to kill Americans." Andrew Higgins and Alan Cullison, "Saga of Dr. Zawahiri Sheds Light on the Roots of al Qaeda Terror," *Wall Street Journal*, July 2, 2002.

47. Bill Clinton, *My Life* (New York: Knopf, 2004), p. 797.

48. "Bin Ladin Creates New Front against US, Israel, Islamabad," *The News in English* (Islamabad), May 28, 1998, p. 12; Foreign Broadcast Information Service Report, "Compilation of Usama Bin Ladin Statements, 1994–January 2004," pp. 68–69. For "the so-called superpower that is America," see "Time magazine interview, January 11, 1999"; "Compilation of Usama Bin Ladin Statements, " p. 98; and PBS, "Osama bin Laden v. The U.S.: Edicts and Statements," April 1999, http://www.pbs.org/wgbh/pages/frontline/shows/binladen/who/edicts.html; and Scheuer, *Osama bin Laden*, p. 129.

49. PBS *Frontline*, "Interview: Osama bin Laden," (May 1998)," http://www.pbs.org/wgbh/pages/frontline/shows/binladen/who/interview.html.

50. In August 2001, O'Neill quit the FBI to head security at the World Trade Center, where his remains were recovered after 9/11. For snippets of O'Neill's conversations with Jean-Charles Brisard, author of a study of terrorist financing for a French intelligence agency, see Anthony Summers and Robbyn Swan, *The Eleventh Day: The Full Story of 9/11* (New York: Ballantine Books, 2011), p. 396.

51. The officials said the Saudis would rather sell their securities than acquiesce. Martin Tolchin, "Foreigners' Political Roles in U.S. Grow by Investing," *New York Times*, December 30, 1985.

52. Bush also described Saudi Prince Bandar, longtime Saudi ambassador to America, as "a friend of mine since Dad's presidency." George W. Bush, *Decision Points* (New York: Crown Publishers, 2010), pp. 403, 247.

53. In a 2003 profile of Bandar in *The New Yorker,* Elsa Walsh wrote that Tenet showed up at Bandar's home during the interview. For more on the friendship, see James Risen, *State of War,* p. 188.

54. That quote from the 9/11 Commission came from a former National Security Council official. See *The 9/11 Commission Report,* chap. 7, "Al Haramain Case Study," p. 116.

55. Risen, *State of War,* p. 181. According to Michael Scheuer, head the CIA's bin Laden unit, the Saudis refused to help perhaps because they wanted to protect themselves from U.S. investigations into their private collaboration with bin Laden in the past. See Coll, *The Bin Ladens,* pp. 436–37.

56. On Tenet and Clarke's objections, see Lawrence Wright, *The Looming Tower,* p. 291. On Tenet's trip to the kingdom, see p. 266.

57. Ibid., p. 267.

58. Risen, *State of War,* pp. 183–84.

59. Bush, *Decision Points,* p. 191.

60. Clinton also admits, however, that Americans had to absorb the news of the strike and his grand jury testimony into his "personal behavior." See Bill Clinton, *My Life* (New York: Knopf, 2004), p. 797. For the quote on Somalia, see p. 804.

61. Ibid., p. 797. The Aldrich Ames case had also done "severe damage" to the CIA, according to Clinton's recollection of Tenet's concern. See p. 818.

62. PBS *Frontline,* "In Search of Al Qaeda," interview with Ahmad Zaidan, http://www.pbs.org/wgbh/pages/frontline/shows/search/interviews/zaidan.html. Reporter Peter Bergen also recounts Zaidan's meeting with al Qaeda member Mohammed Atef after the attack on the USS *Cole,* who said how the group wanted America to react: "We did [the USS] *Cole* [attack] and we wanted the United States to react. And if they reacted, they are going to invade Afghanistan and that's what we want.... We want them to come to our country.... And then we will start holy war against the Americans, exactly like the Soviets." Peter L. Bergen, *The Osama bin Laden I Know: An Oral History of al Qaeda's Leader* (New York: Free Press, 2006), p. 255.

63. Wright, *The Looming Tower,* p. 46.

64. For Kurtz, see Summers, *The Eleventh Day,* p. 286. For Clarke, see Bob Graham, *Intelligence Matters: The CIA, the FBI, Saudi Arabia, and the Failure of America's War on Terror* (New York: Random House, 2004), pp. 136–37.

65. Seymour M. Hersh, "King's Ransom: How Vulnerable Are the Saudi Royals?" *The New Yorker,* October 22, 2001; "Kidnap Team Stalks Ex-U.N. Envoy: Saudi Diplomat is Terror Target," *New York Post,* August 1, 1994; U.S. Department of State, "Saudi Arabia and Human Rights Practices, 1994," February 1995, http://dosfan.lib.uic.edu/ERC/democracy/1994_hrp_report/94hrp_report_nea/SaudiArabia.html; Summers, *The Eleventh Day,* p. 392. At the time, FBI Director Louie Freeh did not use email, an aversion to computers that may have explained his reluctance to update the FBI's computer system or develop a central counterterrorism database. Prince Bandar hired Freeh to be his legal representative after he retired from the bureau. See the full program: PBS *Frontline,* "Black Money," April 7, 2009, http://www.pbs.org/wgbh/pages/frontline/blackmoney/view/.

66. Lisa Myers, "The Missed Opportunities of 9/11: Could the Attacks on America Have Been Disrupted or Delayed?" *NBS News,* July 26, 2004, http://www.nbcnews.com

/id/5469870/#.Ur7N2fRDs50; Anthony Barnet, Lee Hanno, and Martin Bright, "UK Spymasters Shrugged off al-Qaeda 'Recruit's Warning,'" *The Guardian* (London), June 6, 2006, http://www.theguardian.com/world/2004/jun/06/september11.terrorism; Summers, *The Eleventh Day*, pp. 294, 302–03.

67. One future hijacker lived for four months with an informant. For more, see Office of the Inspector General, *A Review of the FBI's handling of Intelligence Information Related to the September 11 Attacks* (Washington: Department of Justice, 2004), http://www.justice.gov/oig/special/s0606/final.pdf, p. 335; and Graham, *Intelligence Matters*, pp. 160–61, 164–65, 168–69, 204.

68. Omar al-Bayoumi was employed by the Saudi Presidency of Civil Aviation from 1975 until 1995 and later paid by a Saudi company that contracted with the Saudi government. See *A Review of the FBI's Handling of Intelligence Information Related to the September 11 Attacks*, p. 331.

69. Ibid., p. 332.

70. Ibid., p. 334.

71. Risen, *State of War*, p. 181.

72. *A Review of the FBI's Handling of Intelligence Information Related to the September 11 Attacks*, pp. 361, 247–48. FBI sources who spoke to Lawrence Wright offered a range of explanations for why the CIA had intelligence but neglected to provide it: the CIA feared that FBI prosecutions might compromise relations with foreign services; the FBI was too clumsy to be trusted with sensitive intelligence; and—more cynically—the CIA, desperate for a source inside al Qaeda to recruit, was running a joint venture with Saudi intelligence. See Wright, *The Looming Tower*, pp. 310–13.

73. *A Review of the FBI's Handling of Intelligence Information Related to the September 11 Attacks*, pp. 315, 361.

74. The full quote by Bob Kerrey (D-NE) was that, of the "three big failures, mistakes" made in the Clinton and Bush administrations after 1998, one was with "allowing al Qaeda to come inside the United States. . . . We continued to allow them to come to the United States; we didn't put a full-scale effort on with consular offices and INS and FBI and all sorts of other people in the United States to try to prevent them from coming into the United States." See "National Commission on Terrorist Attacks upon the United States, Tenth Public Hearing," April 13, 2004, http://www.9-11commission.gov/archive/hearing10/9-11Commission_Hearing_2004-04-13.htm.

75. Mihdhar had already returned to the United States in early July 2001. See *A Review of the FBI's Handling of Intelligence Information Related to the September 11 Attacks*, p. 302; Wright, *The Looming Tower*, pp. 310–13; and Summers, *The Eleventh Day*, p. 384.

76. Barton Gellman, "U.S. Was Foiled Multiple Times in Effort to Capture Bin Laden or Have Him Killed," *Washington Post*, October 3, 2001, http://www.washingtonpost.com/wp-dyn/content/article/2006/06/09/AR2006060900911_pf.html.

77. Richard A. Clarke, "Memorandum for Condoleezza Rice," National Security Council January 25, 2001, http://www2.gwu.edu/~nsarchiv/NSAEBB/NSAEBB343/osama_bin_laden_file09.pdf. Emphasis in the original.

78. Reference to President's Daily Brief, "Bin Laden Determined to Strike in US," Central Intelligence Agency (CIA), August 6, 2001, (declassified and publicly released on April 10, 2004), http://nsarchive.gwu.edu/NSAEBB/NSAEBB343/osama_bin_laden_file02.pdf. President Bush later claimed the CIA "could not confirm any concrete plans." See Bush, *Decision Points*, p. 135.

79. Philip Shenon, *The Commission: The Uncensored History of the 9/11 Investigation* (New York: Hachette Book Group, 2008), p. 247. See also Lisa Myers, "Did Ashcroft Brush off Terror Warnings?" *NBS News*, June 22, 2004.

80. "Ashcroft Flying High," *CBSNews.com*, July 26, 2001; "Bin Laden Determined to Strike in US."

81. In Bandar's company, Bush cut off one reporter who began to raise the subject of 9/11. See Summers, *The Eleventh Day*, p. 406.

82. The FBI had interviewed some, but not all, of the departing Saudis. No doubt many were likely innocent of any crime, but U.S. government documents reveal that the FBI was uncertain as to whether those who left had information pertinent to the 9/11 investigation. Summers, *The Eleventh Day*, p. 406.

83. "Joint Inquiry into Intelligence Community Activities before and after the Terrorist Attacks of September 11, 2001," House Permanent Select Committee on Intelligence and Senate Select Committee on Intelligence, 107th Cong., 2nd sess., S. Rep. 107-351 and H. Rep. 107-792, http://www.gpoaccess.gov/serialset/creports/pdf/fullreport_errata.pdf.

84. Josh Meyer, "Report Links Saudi Government to 9/11 Hijackers, Sources Say," *Los Angeles Times*, August 2, 2003; James Risen and David Johnson, "Report on September 11 Suggests a Role by Saudi Spies," *New York Times*, August 2, 2003; Mike Allex, "Bush Won't Release Classified September 11 Report," *Washington Post*, July 30, 2003; David Johnson and Douglas Jehl, "Bush Refuses to Declassify Saudi Section of Report," *New York Times*, July 30, 2003.

85. Dana Priest, "White House, CIA Kept Key Portions of Report Classified," *Washington Post*, July 25, 2003; Helen Kennedy, "New Rage Over 9/11 & Saudis Pols Get Censored Report," *New York Daily News*, July 25, 2003.

86. Graham, *Intelligence Matters*, p. 215.

87. Summers, *The Eleventh Day*, p. 416.

88. "Ex-Saudi Ambassador: Kingdom Could Have Helped U.S. Prevent 9/11," *CNN.com*, November 2, 2007, http://www.cnn.com/2007/WORLD/meast/11/01/saudiarabia.terrorism/index.html.

89. Risen, *State of War*, p. 181.

90. Ibid. Steve Coll cites the head of the CIA's bin Laden unit, Michael Scheuer, as the one who submitted the request to the Kingdom of Saudi Arabia for basic information about Osama bin Laden. The agency received no reply. See Coll, *The Bin Ladens*, pp. 416–17.

91. Alex Strick van Linschoten and Felix Kuehn, *An Enemy We Created: The Myth of the Taliban-/Al Qaeda Merger in Afghanistan, 1970–2010* (New York: Oxford University Press, 2012), p. 165; Summers and Swan, *The Eleventh Day*, pp. 393–94.

92. Risen, *State of War*, p. 182.

93. Some in the CIA had also begun to suspect that the highly classified intelligence and communications intercepts it was sharing with GID were being passed to al Qaeda. See Risen, *State of War*, p. 182.

94. Richard H. Jones, "GOK Sees Strong Saudi Commitment against Terrorism (03KUWAIT4680)," American Embassy in Kuwait, October 14, 2003.

95. Coll, *The Bin Ladens*, p. 437.

96. Henry Kissinger, *Does America Need a Foreign Policy? Toward a Diplomacy for the 21st Century* (New York: Simon and Schuster, 2001), p. 293.

97. Carmen bin Ladin, *Inside the Kingdom: My Life in Saudi Arabia* (New York: Grand Central Publishing, 2004), p. 4.

98. See Summers, *The Eleventh Day*, p. 419.

99. Josh Meyer, "Report Links Saudi Government to 9/11 Hijackers, Sources Say," *Los Angeles Times,* August 2, 2003.

100. State Department, Bureau of Democracy, Human Rights and Labor, "Country Report on Human Rights Practices for 2012: Saudi Arabia," http://www.state.gov/j /drl/rls/hrrpt/humanrightsreport/index.htm?year=2012&dlid=204381 #wrapper.

101. James B. Smith, "Saudi Arabia: General Jones' Jan. 12, 2010 Meeting with Prince Mohammed Bin Naif, Assistant Minister of Interior (10RIYADH90)," American Embassy in Riyadh, January 19, 2010; Lawrence Wright, "The Kingdom of Silence," *The New Yorker,* January 5, 2004.

102. David Ottoway, "The King and Us," *Foreign Affairs* 88, no. 3 (May/June 2009): 121–31, https://www.foreignaffairs.com/articles/middle-east/2009-05-01/king -and-us.

103. Thomas E. Ricks, "Briefing Depicted Saudis as Enemies," *Washington Post,* August 6, 2002; Jack Shafer, "The PowerPoint that Rocked the Pentagon?" *Slate,* August 7, 2002.

104. Kissinger called the embargo an "actual strangulation of the industrialized world" and implied the West had plans to seize Persian Gulf oil militarily. "Kissinger on Oil, Food, and Trade," *Business Week,* January 13, 1975, p. 69; and "Excerpts from the Kissinger News Conference," *New York Times,* November 22, 1973. President Gerald Ford also referred to the embargo as "economic strangulation." See "Gerald Ford: They Will See Something Is Being Done," *Time,* January 20, 1975, p. 21. Defense Secretary James Schlesinger indicated "conceivably military measures in response" in the event of another oil embargo. See "Now a Tougher U.S.: Interview with James R. Schlesinger, Secretary of Defense," *U.S. News and World Report,* May 26, 1975, pp. 26–27. For more articles and essays on this confrontational approach, see Miles Ignotus, "Oil: The Issue of American Intervention," *Commentary,* January 1975; "Seizing Arab Oil," *Harper's,* March 1975; Glen Frankel, "U.S. Mulled Seizing Oil Fields in 1973," *Washington Post,* January 1, 2004; and Owen Bowcott, "UK Feared Americans Would Invade Gulf During 1973 Oil Crisis," *Guardian* (London), January 1, 2004.

105. The Senate Intelligence Committee, in July 2004, concluded there was no Iraq–al Qaeda link, and stated that claims made in the October 2002 National Intelligence Estimate about Iraq's alleged WMD were "either *overstated, or were not supported by, the underlying intelligence reporting.*" [Emphasis added]. The committee later expanded their investigation. See "Report of the Select Committee on Intelligence on the U.S. Intelligence Community's Prewar Intelligence Assessments on Iraq," http://www.intelligence.senate .gov/108301.pdf; "Senate Report on Intelligence Activities Relating to Iraq Conducted by the Policy Counterterrorism Evaluation Group and the Office of Special Plans within the Office of the Under Secretary of Defense for Policy," June 2008, 110th Cong., 2nd sess., http://www.intelligence.senate.gov/080605/phase2b.pdf. The 9/11 Commission also found "no evidence" that Iraq and al Qaeda "ever developed into a collaborative operational relationship." See *The 9/11 Commission Report.* And a declassified 2007 Pentagon investigation concluded that civilians under Secretary of Defense Donald Rumsfeld and Under Secretary of Defense for Policy Douglas Feith "developed, produced, and then disseminated alterative intelligence assessments." Inspector General, United States Department of Defense, "Review of the Pre-Iraqi War Activities of the Office of Under Secretary of Defense for Policy," Report No. 07-Intell-04, February 9, 2007 http://www.fas.org/irp/agency/dod/ig020907-decl.pdf.

106. Robert Baer, *Sleeping with the Devil: How Washington Sold Its Soul for Saudi Crude* (New York: Crown, 2003).

107. *The 9/11 Commission Report,* chap. 7, Al Haramain Case Study.

108. Rachel Bronson, "5 Myths about U.S.-Saudi Relations," *Washington Post,* May 21, 2006, http://www.washingtonpost.com/wp-dyn/content/article/2006/05/19/AR2006051901758_pf.html.

109. Risen, *State of War,* p. 177.

110. U.S. Department of the Treasury, "Additional Al-Haramain Branches, Former Leader Designated by Treasury as Al Qaida Supporters Treasury Marks Latest Action in Joint Designation with Saudia Arabia," press release, June 2, 2004, http://www.treasury.gov/press-center/press-releases/Pages/js1703.aspx.

111. U.S. Department of the Treasury, "U.S.-Based Branch of Al Haramain Foundation Linked to Terror Treasury Designates U.S. Branch, Director," press release, September 9, 2004, http://www.treasury.gov/press-center/press-releases/Pages/js1895.aspx.

112. The quote and core finding is from a 2005 Government Accountability Office report. See "*International Affairs: Information on U.S. Agencies' Efforts to Address Islamic Extremism*" (Washington: GAO, 2005), http://www.gao.gov/assets/250/247784.html.

113. Office of the Under Secretary of Defense, "*Report of the Defense Science Board Task Force on Strategic Communication,*" (Washington: DOD, 2004), http://www.dod.mil/pubs/foi/Science_and_Technology/DSB/05-F-0422.pdf.

114. Council on Foreign Relations, "In Support of Arab Democracy: Why and How," Independent Task Force Report No. 54, June 2005.

115. Richard Wike and Nilanthi Samaranayake, "Where Terrorism Finds Support in the Muslim World," Pew Research Center, May 23, 2006.

116. "Saudi Police 'Stopped' Fire Rescue," March 15, 2002, *BBC.com;* Lawrence Wright, "Kingdom of Silence," *New Yorker,* January 5, 2004.

117. Office of the Director of National Intelligence (ODNI), "Declassified Key Judgments of the National Intelligence Estimate 'Trends in Global Terrorism: Implications for the United States," (Washington, D.C.: Office of the Director of National Intelligence, April 2006), http://www.governmentattic.org/5docs/NIE-2006-02R.pdf.

118. James A. Baker III and Lee H. Hamilton, cochairs, et al., "Iraq Study Group Report," United States Institute of Peace, December 6, 2006), p. 25, http://media.usip.org/reports/iraq_study_group_report.pdf.

119. Christopher M. Blanchard and Alfred B. Prados, "Saudi Arabia: Terrorist Financing Issues," CRS Report for Congress, September 14, 2007; and *The 9/11 Commission Report,* chap. 7, "Al Haramain Case Study." For more on joint U.S.-Saudi efforts against terrorist financing, see testimony of Deputy Assistant Secretary of the Treasury Juan Zarate and Deputy Assistant Director of the FBI Counterterrorism Operational Support Branch Thomas Harrington, U.S. Congress, House of Representatives, Hearing of the Subcommittee on the Middle East and Central Asia of the House Committee on International Relations on "Saudi Arabia and the Fight Against Terrorism Financing." March 24, 2004.

120. U.S. Embassy, Riyadh, Cable 09 Riyadh 496, "Scenesetter for Senator Bond's April 6–8 Visit to Saudi Arabia," March 31, 2009, http://wikileaks.org/cable/2009/03/09RIYADH496.html.

121. "Terrorist Finance: Action Request for Senior Level Engagement on Terrorism Finance," *The Guardian* (London), December 30, 2009, http://www.theguardian.com/world/us-embassy-cables-documents/242073.

122. Ibid. For more on Saudi private and charitable giving inadvertently going to militant groups, see the analysis of former FBI counterterrorism intelligence analyst Matthew Levitt, "Stemming the Flow of Terrorist Financing: Practical and Conceptual Challenges," *The Fletcher Forum of World Affairs* 27, no. 1 (Winter/Spring 2003): 59–70, http://ui04e.moit.tufts.edu/forum/archives/pdfs/27-1pdfs/Levitt3.pdf. See also, "Charitable and Humanitarian Organizations in the Network of International Terrorist Financing," testimony of Matthew A. Levitt before the Subcommittee on International Trade and Finance, Committee on Banking, Housing, and Urban Affairs, United States Senate (August 1, 2002), http://www.washingtoninstitute.org/media/levitt/levitt080102.htm; and Matthew A. Levitt, "Tackling the Financing of Terrorism in Saudi Arabia," The Washington Institute for Near East Policy, Policy Watch #609, March 11, 2002, http://www.washingtoninstitute.org/watch/index.htm.

123. Government Accountability Office, "Combating Terrorism: U.S. Agencies Report Progress Countering Terrorism and Its Financing in Saudi Arabia, but Continued Focus on Counter Terrorism Financing Efforts Needed," September 24, 2009, http://www.gao.gov/assets/300/295873.pdf.

124. United States Department of State, Bureau for International Narcotics and Law Enforcement Affairs, "International Narcotics Control Strategy Report: Volume II Money Laundering and Financial Crimes," March 2009, p. 435, http://www.state.gov/documents/organization/120055.pdf.

125. Quote from U.S. Embassy Riyadh, in a cable dated March 22, 2009, "Counterterrorism Adviser Brennan's Meeting with Saudi King Abdullah," https://wikileaks.org/plusd/cables/09RIYADH447_a.html.

126. Freedom House, "Freedom in the World 2010: Global Erosion of Freedom," January 12, 2010, http://www.freedomhouse.org/article/freedom-world-2010-global-erosion-freedom.

127. A former high-ranking official on Middle East policy in the Clinton administration contended that the Saudis saw the Obama administration as a threat to their domestic security. Martin Indyk, "Amid the Arab Spring, Obama's Dilemma over Saudi Arabia," *Washington Post*, April 8, 2011.

128. The *Los Angeles Times* spoke of the "longtime allies" being "put on a collision course" by regional upheavals. Paul Richter and Neela Banerjee, "U.S.-Saudi Rivalry Intensifies," *Los Angeles Times*, June 19, 2011.

129. U.S. Embassy, Riyadh, "Scenesetter for Secretary Clinton's Feb. 15–16 Visit to Saudi Arabia (10RIYADH178)," February 11, 2010, http://wikileaks.org/cable/2010/02/10RIYADH178.html.

130. Prince Turki and other Saudi leaders feared an Iranian SCUD missile could hit Saudi oil facilities and warned U.S. diplomats that Gulf countries might be compelled to station nuclear weapons as a deterrent. On nuclear weapons, see Scott Mcgehee, "Saudi Exchange with Russian Ambassador on Iran's Nuclear Plans," American Embassy in Riyadh, January 28, 2009, http://www.theguardian.com/world/us-embassy-cables-documents/189229]. On fears of SCUD missile strikes, see U.S. Embassy, Riyadh, "APHSCT Townsend's November 16 Meeting with Saudi NSA Bandar Bin Sultan on Iranian Threats (06RIYADH9095)," December 16, 2006, https://wikileaks.org/plusd/cables/06RIYADH9095_a.html; and U.S. Embassy, Riyadh, "APHSCT Townsend February 6 Meeting with Foreign Minister Prince Saud Al-Faisal (07RIYADH367)," February 24, 2007, https://www.wikileaks.org/plusd/cables/07RIYADH367_a.html.

131. "Security Council Al-Qaida Sanctions Committee: Amends 111 Entries on its Sanctions List," December 13, 2011, http://www.un.org/News/Press/docs//2011/sc10483.doc.htm.

132. Sally Jacobs, David Filipov, and Patricia Wen, "The Fall of the House of Tsarnaev," *Boston Globe*, December 15, 2013, http://www.bostonglobe.com/Page/Boston/2011-2020/WebGraphics/Metro/BostonGlobe.com/2013/12/15tsarnaev/tsarnaev.html.

133. Tim Lister and Paul Cruickshank, "Older Brother in Boston Bombings Grew Increasingly Religious, Analysis Shows," *CNN.com*, April 20, 2013.

134. Ksenia Svetlova, "The Saudi Connection Linking the Boston Marathon to September 11," *Ha'aretz* (Tel Aviv), April 20, 2013; "Boston Bombing Suspect Tamerlan Tsarnaev's Wife Katherine Russell 'Had No Idea of Plot,'" *Courier-Mail* (Brisbane), April 25, 2013.

135. Alexei Vassiliev, *The History of Saudi Arabia* (New York: New York University Press, 2000), p. 473.

136. Experts also report Salafism's spread to Mali, a former democratic U.S. ally overthrown by domestic insurgency, military coup, and fighters with weapons from Libya following the 2011 NATO invasion. Antoine Basbous, head of the Paris-based Observatory of Arab Countries, said "the Salafism we hear about in Mali and North Africa is in fact the export version of Wahhabism." See Antoine Basbous, quoted in Marc Daou, "How Saudi Petrodollars Fuel Rise of Salafism," *France 24* (Paris), September 30, 2012, http://www.france24.com/en/20120929-how-saudi-arabia-petrodollars-finance-salafist-winter-islamism-wahhabism-egypt/; Robin Wright, "Don't Fear Islamists, Fear Salafis," *New York Times*, August 19, 2012.

137. "Ibid.

138. Khaled Yacoub Oweis, "Insight: Saudi Arabia boosts Salafist rivals to al Qaeda in Syria," Reuters, October 1, 2013.

139. U.S. Department of Defense, "Contracts: Press Operations, No: 593-13," August 20, 2013, http://www.defense.gov/contracts/contract.aspx?contractid=5116; U.S. Department of State, "Cluster Munitions," http://www.state.gov/t/pm/wra/c25930.htm.

140. Richard Miniter, "Saudis Lament, 'We Have Been Stabbed in the Back by Obama,'" *FoxNews.com*, December 27, 2013.

141. "The Situation Room," April 23, 2009, http://transcripts.cnn.com/TRANSCRIPTS/0904/23/sitroom.02.html; Robin Wright, "Don't Fear Islamists, Fear Salafis," *New York Times*, August 19, 2012. Emphasis in original.

142. Ambassador Chas Freeman attributes that problem to 2001 peace talks. See *Ten Years After 9/11: Managing U.S.-Saudi Relations* (Washington: Carnegie Endowment for International Peace, 2011), http://carnegieendowment.org/files/91211_transcript_SaudiPanelTwo.pdf.

143. Summer Said and Benoit Faucon, "Shale Threatens Saudi Economy, Warns Prince Alwaleed," *Wall Street Journal*, July 29, 2013.

About the Authors

Ted Galen Carpenter is senior fellow for defense and foreign policy studies at the Cato Institute. He is the author of 10 books and the contributing editor of 10 on international affairs, including *Perilous Partners: The Benefits and Pitfalls of America's Alliances with Authoritarian Regimes* (coauthored with Malou Innocent), *The Fire Next Door: Mexico's Drug Violence and the Danger to America*, *Smart Power: Toward a Prudent Foreign Policy for America*, and *The Captive Press: Foreign Policy Crises and the First Amendment*.

His forthcoming book, *Gullible Superpower: U.S. Support for Bogus Foreign Democratic Movements*, will be published in February 2019.

Malou Innocent is an adjunct scholar at the Cato Institute. She was a foreign policy analyst at Cato from 2007 to 2013. She is a member of the International Institute for Strategic Studies, and her primary research interests include Middle East and Persian Gulf security issues and U.S. foreign policy toward Pakistan, Afghanistan, and China. With Ted Galen Carpenter, she is the author of *Perilous Partners: The Benefits and Pitfalls of America's Alliances with Authoritarian Regimes* (Cato Institute, 2015).

Cato Institute

Founded in 1977, the Cato Institute is a public policy research foundation dedicated to broadening the parameters of policy debate to allow consideration of more options that are consistent with the principles of limited government, individual liberty, and peace. To that end, the Institute strives to achieve greater involvement of the intelligent, concerned lay public in questions of policy and the proper role of government.

The Institute is named for *Cato's Letters,* libertarian pamphlets that were widely read in the American Colonies in the early 18th century and played a major role in laying the philosophical foundation for the American Revolution.

Despite the achievement of the nation's Founders, today virtually no aspect of life is free from government encroachment. A pervasive intolerance for individual rights is shown by government's arbitrary intrusions into private economic transactions and its disregard for civil liberties. And while freedom around the globe has notably increased in the past several decades, many countries have moved in the opposite direction, and most governments still do not respect or safeguard the wide range of civil and economic liberties.

To address those issues, the Cato Institute undertakes an extensive publications program on the complete spectrum of policy issues. Books, monographs, and shorter studies are commissioned to examine the federal budget, Social Security, regulation, military spending, international trade, and myriad other issues. Major policy conferences are held throughout the year, from which papers are published thrice yearly in the *Cato Journal.* The Institute also publishes the quarterly magazine *Regulation.*

In order to maintain its independence, the Cato Institute accepts no government funding. Contributions are received from foundations, corporations, and individuals, and other revenue is generated from the sale of publications. The Institute is a nonprofit, tax-exempt, educational foundation under Section 501(c)3 of the Internal Revenue Code.

CATO INSTITUTE
1000 Massachusetts Ave., N.W.
Washington, D.C. 20001
www.cato.org

www.ingramcontent.com/pod-product-compliance
Lightning Source LLC
Chambersburg PA
CBHW022340280326
41934CB00006B/705